Bicycling Guide to the Lake Michigan Trail

FOREWORD

You won't be disappointed in your choice to experience Lake Michigan by bicycle. From sandy beaches to bustling cities; from scenic lake shore vistas to tree lined quiet roads; as a cyclist this could be the best bicycle tourism route you'll ever experience.

This route has it all; available services, tourism towns, bicycle trails, low traffic roads, connections to rail (Amtrak) and airports, and a variety of historic and cultural experiences that will make the trip come to life. Cyclists have so many options on Lake Michigan; choose to bike for a few days along sections of the Lake that appeal to you or go for the full loop experience. There are two national lakeshores – Indiana Dunes and Sleeping Bear Dunes, both excellent examples of how national parks are welcoming and encouraging cyclists to experience parks outside the car. There are quaint tourism communities across the entirety of the route with bed and breakfast accommodations, state and local parks and a growing number of bike trails and lanes that make riding easy. There also exists an abundance of opportunities to enjoy the Lake off the bicycle. Take a ferry ride, rent a canoe or sea kayak, stroll the sleepy lakeshore towns, or just enjoy a day at the beach.

Bob's Bicycling Guide to Lake Michigan couldn't come at a better time. Many of the routes Bob recommends in this book are now part of a national project called the U.S. Bicycle Route System (USBRS). The system is numbered, signed and supported by numerous agencies and bicycle/trail advocates at the local and state level. Look for signs showing U.S. Bike Routes 35, 36, 37 and 10 (the signing project is ongoing and will take time to complete). As the national coordinator for USBRS, I've seen growing enthusiasm for people-powered tourism. I think you will find the route delightful and the people welcoming.

Enjoy!

Ginny Sullivan
Director of Travel Initiatives
Coordinator of the U.S. Bicycle Route System
Adventure Cycling Association

D0905586

Bicycling Guide to the Lake Michigan Trail

Published by
Spirits Creek
Fort Smith, Arkansas

Edited by Nancy Raney

All photographs by Bob Robinson, unless otherwise stated.

Cover photo was taken at the White River Light Station Museum, located at White Hall, Michigan. I am waiting to witness what is said to be one of the best sunsets in the world.

Library of Congress Control Number: 2014907048

ISBN 978-0-9818952-2-2

Contents

This book is dedicated to anyone who has ever selected a bicycle as their preferred vehicle of travel.

Acknowledgments:

I would like to express my appreciation to the following people who contributed to this book: Nancy Raney, Ginny Sullivan, Nathaniel Benoit, Nancy Tibbett, Demian March, Rich Moeller, Josh DeBruyn, David Hart, Saara Snow, Judy Lansky, Dan Hudec, Kerry Irons, Sharon Cole, Rich Moeller, Demian March, and Robee Burian. I could not have written the book without them. I also would like to recognize the Michigan Department of Transportation, Wisconsin Department of Transportation, Bicycle Federation of Wisconsin, Bicycle Indiana Org, Michigan Trails and Greenways Alliance, League of Michigan Bicyclists, Northwest Indiana Regional Planning Committe, and Adventure Cycling Association.

I thank you all.

Introduction

When I finished writing Bicycling Guide to the Mississippi River Trail I began the search for my next project. I bicycled the west coast, thinking that would be a good route to document. It was a fun ride; however I decided against writing a guidebook for it. Several years, as well as many cycling tours later, I still had yet to find a bicycle route to document in another guidebook. Until one day, when I had the atlas out planning a trip and there it was jumping out at me like the natural wonder that it is, Lake Michigan. I said to myself, "Now that would be a sweet ride." And I can now truthfully say, "Yes, it is a sweet ride."

Utilizing bike paths and bicycle friendly highways based on information collected from the Northwest Indiana Regional Planning Committee, Wisconsin Department of Transportation, Bicycle Federation Wisconsin, Michigan Department of Transportation, League of Michigan Bicyclists, and Adventure Cycling Association this guidebook documents a continuous 1,200 plus mile bicycle-friendly route around Lake Michigan. The guidebook also includes services, lodging, camping, and other valuable resources that help contribute to a successful and enjoyable cycling experience.

The Lake Michigan Trail (LMT) routes cyclists though dense hardwood forests, along sandy beaches, and across tall bluffs offering scenic views across this great body of water. With the lake being over 300 miles long and over 100 miles wide, and with large surf lapping onto its sandy shores, I was often reminded of bicycling along the west coast.

The LMT has something for everyone. In Chicago the route gives cyclists the option of skirting the metropolis on the 18 mile Lake Front Trail, or venturing less than a block off of this separated paved path to reach Chicago's downtown district, for a truly cosmopolitan experience. The LMT also courses along quiet country roads, like those in the Door Peninsula. Where, due to its physical isolation, the area has preserved an easy going way of life from a much simpler period in time. The Door Peninsula, and both Michigan's Upper Peninsula and its eastern lakeshores have been catering to visitors for over a century, so they are well equipped to handle the needs of bicycle tourists.

A big plus for cyclists riding the LMT is that it is a loop tour, so you don't have to plan a shuttle back to your vehicle. If you do not have time for a tour around the entire lake, you can split it up by hitching a ride across Lake Michigan on ferries between Milwaukee, WI and Muskegon, MI, and Manitowoc, WI and Ludington, MI.

I recorded the services which I believed would best serve the needs of cyclists, however, if anyone discovers lodging or services that they believe to be more accommodating to cyclists, please email the information to bob@spiritscreek.com. I will list this, along with other updates, on my website http://spiritscreek.com/ to provide everyone with the most up-to-date information available before beginning their LMT Adventure! Also, upon completing your LMT Adventure, email me and I will send you a certification of completion. Enjoy your LMT Adventure!

Using This Guide

This guidebook is not a personal journal of my adventures while riding the LMT. Rather, it is a collection of relevant materials for cyclists to use to create their own adventure around Lake Michigan.

The guidebook is divided into sections that progress clockwise around Lake Michigan. The mileage for each section is not based on the number of miles cyclists should ride each day. Not all cyclists share the same agenda. Instead, each section provides the materials a cyclist needs to create their own daily schedule, and the flexibility to adjust their schedule as needed. Each section includes text, services, a map, and the all-important Mileage Log, which lists turn-by-turn directions. When using this material, I suggest that you first read the text associated with a section, to familiarize yourself with the route, and any attractions along the way. The services included will help you select a target destination for the day's ride, and the map will provide an overall understanding of the route. Be sure to read the Mileage Log to familiarize yourself with the turns involved in the first part of your ride, and keep it handy as a reference throughout your trip.

Now get on your bike and create Your Own Lake Michigan Trail Adventure!

Text

The text provides a running account of each route in its associated section, and points out many of its attractions. It often relates to the history of the area, so that cyclists can better appreciate the communities and scenery along the way. When needed, the text also serves to complement the Mileage Log, by providing greater detail for complicated directions or other potential hazards.

At the first use of an acronym within the text I will explain it's meaning, such as (Lake Michigan Trail) LMT. So if you encounter an unknown acronym, thumb back a page or two to locate it's meaning. The guidebook does not identify every attraction that the LMT passes. There remain many more attractoins for you to discover on your own.

Services

Where services are available, each section in the guide lists camping, lodging, and bike shops. Every possible lodging, etc. is not listed. Those services that are preceded by an asterisk (*) are located immediately along the route.

Mileage Log

Column headings:

Miles N/S: Accumulated miles for the referenced section, when riding clockwise around the lake.

Directions: Instructions and points of interest along the route. Rows beginning with an * are intended as an FYI, such as a town or a turn for an optional side trip.

Dist: The distance in miles to travel for the associated instruction.

R: Rating for traffic & road condtions, usng a scale of 1 ideal and 5 very congested, and P for separated paved path.

Services: C= camping, G = a full grocery store, L = lodging, such as a motel, bed-and-breakfast, lodge, etc., Q = a type of business where cyclists can stop for a quick snack, such as a convenience store, small grocery, etc. R = a restaurant that serves prepared foods. Available services will be listed both for the section of road that they are on, and the town they are located in.

Miles S/N: Reversed accumulated miles for the referenced section, for cyclists traveling counter clockwise around the lake.

Acronyms used in the Mileage Log directions:

CR: County Road, L: Left, R: Right, SH: State Highway, SL: Stop Light, SS: Stop Sign, YS: Yield Sign.

MAP KEY

🚲 —— LMT Route	☐ County road
—— Non-LMT highway	◯ State highway
US highway	▲ Camping
Interstate highway	☐ Monument

Equipment

If you have a bike, you can tour. My first bicycle tour was on a 10-speed Huffy® with a daypack strapped to a bolt-on rack. I do admit that touring is a lot more enjoyable with my Fuji® Touring bike and Jandd® Large Mountain Panniers. So, if you would like to improve the chances of your first tour being an enjoyable experience, I recommend that you read one of the many books written specifically about preparation for bicycle touring. Visit the Adventure Cycling Association website for a list of available publications.

Just don't allow your equipment to stop your adventure.

Safety

The list of the roads described in this guidebook as the designated route of the Lake Michigan Trail, is not an indication that they are safe for cyclists. When you ride the roads described in this book, you assume responsibility for your own safety. Most of the route of the Lake Michigan Tour follows highways that are used by motor vehicles, and dangers that are normally associated with riding such roads exist while riding the Lake Michigan Trail.

Weather: Average High/Low/Rainfall

City, State	Jan Hi Lo Rn	Feb Hi Lo Rn	Mar Hi Lo Rn	Apr Hi Lo Rn	May Hi Lo Rn	Jun Hi Lo Rn	Jul Hi Lo Rn	Aug Hi Lo Rn	Sep Hi Lo Rn	Oct Hi Lo Rn	Nov Hi Lo Rn	Dec Hi Lo Rn
New Buffalo, MI	31 18 2.68	35 21 2.43	46 30 2.94	59 40 3.59	70 50 4.00	79 60 4.17	82 64 4.27	81 63 4.27	74 55 3.61	62 44 3.69	48 34 3.99	35 23 3.17
Milwaukee, WI	29 16 1.76	33 19 1.71	42 28 2.27	54 37 3.56	65 47 3.40	75 57 3.90	80 64 3.67	79 63 3.97	71 55 3.18	59 43 2.65	46 32 2.71	33 20 2.71
Sturgeon Bay, WI	26 10 1.65	29 13 1.31	39 22 1.94	52 33 2.75	64 43 3.14	74 53 3.64	79 59 3.38	77 58 3.47	70 51 3.36	56 39 3.05	43 29 2.49	30 17 1.82
Escanaba, MI	26 06 1.06	29 07 0.97	36 16 1.77	48 29 2.23	60 40 2.94	70 50 2.98	76 55 3.37	75 55 3.35	68 47 3.20	55 36 2.96	42 25 2.45	31 13 1.44
St. Ignace, MI	26 13 1.74	29 13 1.49	36 20 1.57	49 31 1.88	61 42 2.50	70 52 2.73	75 58 2.54	75 59 2.73	68 52 3.16	55 41 3.44	43 31 2.39	31 21 1.80
Traverse City, MI	28 15 2.82	31 15 1.55	40 22 1.86	54 32 2.78	66 42 2.59	76 52 3.16	80 56 3.02	78 57 3.38	70 50 3.53	57 39 3.22	44 30 2.70	32 21 2.49
Muskegon, MI	31 20 2.03	33 21 1.91	43 27 2.25	56 37 2.91	67 47 3.25	76 57 2.55	81 62 2.37	79 61 3.39	71 53 3.89	59 43 3.11	46 34 3.36	35 25 2.55

Lake Michigan Trail
SECTION 1

New Buffalo to Oak Ridge Prairie Park (44 miles)

New Buffalo, MI was selected as the starting point in this guide to give cyclists a day or so to loosen up before reaching any major populated areas. New Buffalo has also traditionally been known as "The Gateway to Michigan." With the tour around Lake Michigan being a loop, cyclists can skip through the guidebook to begin at whatever location is convenient.

You might choose to arrive a day or two early to enjoy New Buffalo's beach and quaint village atmosphere before beginning your epic cycling adventure.

When you are ready to begin your ride follow the Mileage Log to head south out of town, on historic US 12. Before the creation of I-94 this was once a popular route was known as "Chicago Road", linking Detroit and Chicago. For motorists from the northeastern states this was an extension of Route 66 on their migration west. The roots for the route itself date back to Native Americans, when the same general route followed a path known then as the "Sauk Trail."

If you are hauling your bicycle to the start in your vehicle and need a place to leave your car during the tour, Robee Burian, at Judy's Motel and Campground, said he will be glad to store it. The establishment has been meeting the needs of travelers since the heyday of the Chicago Road and the family-owned business is now operating under the management of its third generation.

The lodging I have listed in the guidebook for New Buffalo are clean motels and conveniently located along the LMT route, however, if you would prefer a newer place to stay, continue east on South Whittaker Street for a couple of miles to the I94 ramp, and you will find a wide selection of franchise motels.

Exiting Grand Beach Road you ride under the stately white "Grand Beach" arch that has been welcoming visitors to the beach resort area since the early 1900s. These beach resort communities are the first of many you will ride through on your tour around Lake Michigan. Over the years the communities you ride through in this area are no longer equipped primarily to accommodate the needs of temporary visitors. The roads you ride here are bordered by cottages for the "some-time" and "full-time" overflow population of nearby Chicago.

These residential roads make for a pleasant ride, frequently bordered by beautiful beaches on one side and an interesting mix of old and new architecture on the other. There are also several points along this route with public access to the beach for your

A view of the wetlands alongside the Oak Savannah Trail

inaugural swim in the clear waters of Lake Michigan. Many of these stops also have restrooms and tables for you to pause to watch the sailboats silently gliding across the surface of the glistening waters of the lake.

Upon your approach to Michigan City on Franklin Street, use caution when riding the metal grid of the historic Trail Creek drawbridge. You might consider using the sidewalk.

The main route skirts the border of Michigan City, but the area has an interesting history. If you would like to learn more about the area, continue riding Franklin Street another three miles to reach the LaPorte County Convention and Visitors Bureau, at 4073 Franklin Street for more information.

Leaving Michigan City, once again on US 12, you pass a sign

stating that you are entering Indiana Dunes National Lakeshore. Shortly after this, when the route veers right on Beverly Drive, if you remain on US 12 another half mile you reach the parking lot for the Calumet Trail. This is a gravel path that parallels a railroad track. Later, the route described in this guide does utilize a section of the Calumet Trail, so if you would like to avoid riding on the highway and don't mind riding on gravel, you have the option to begin using the trail at this point. You also have the option to remain on US 12, which parallels Calumet Trail. However traffic on US 12 can be busy at times, so the guide generally avoids it when possible.

If you plan to camp at the Dunewood Campground, while riding Lake Front Drive you need to keep an eye out for Broadway Road. You will need to turn left here and ride a little over a mile to reach the campground.

When the Mileage Log does route cyclists on the Calumet Trail, if you would prefer to avoid riding on gravel completely, continue straight on E State Park Road to reach US 12, which parallels the trail.

The Calumet Trail passes the South Shoreline Dune Park Station, located at the entrance to Indiana Dunes State Park. Cyclists flying in on one of Chicago's airports might want to utilize the train for quick transportation either to/from this or the station in New Buffalo. There are also commuter trains heading north out of Chicago, for those who are riding around Lake Michigan in stages, and want to skip to a point where their previous tour ended. After writing the Bicycling Guide to the Mississippi River Trail, I received an email from a man who was riding the entire route in two or three day segments, and having the ride of his life. The Lake Michigan route is even better suited to be ridden in separate independent segments. I'm sure a lot of cyclists who don't have an extended period of time will take advantage of this.

In Chesterton, you might want to turn left off 15th Street on Broadway to get something to eat before heading out on the Duneland Trail. There aren't many opportunities for food once you're on the trail. I did find one place at the Willowcreek Road crossing, where you can turn left to go eat at "Tate's Place."

I enjoyed riding through the residential lakeshore areas, but it was nice to begin riding Duneland's paved separated trails. The wooded buffer zone alongside the trail provides a great outdoor experience, with squirrels racing alongside your bike and always the possibilities for other wildlife encounters.

There are not many dining choices along the designated route through Hobart. If you are in need of loading up on some calories, rather than turning left on Georgianna Street, continue straight on 3rd Street about a half mile to reach downtown Hobart.

The Oak Savannah Trail takes you across wooden bridges through some picturesque wetland habitats, offering great waterfowl viewing opportunities and "photo ops." When the trail crosses Liverpool Road, at the John Robertson Park, you can turn left and ride about a mile then turn right on W 61st Avenue. for another tenth of a mile to reach the motels listed for Merrillville. You will also have several choices of eating establishments in the immediate area.

Camping

*Judy's Motel & CG
18891 W US 12
New Buffalo, MI
269-469-0222

Dunewood CG
437 E Goldwood
Michigan City, IN
219-395-1882w

*Indiana Dunes Natl SP
1600 N 25 E
Chesterton, IN
219-926-1952

Lodging

*Buffalo Motel
18373 US 12
New Buffalo, MI
269-469-0846

*Grand Beach Motel
19189 US 12
New Buffalo, MI
269-469-1555

Gray Goose Inn B&B
350 Indiana Boundary Rd
Chesterton, IN
219-926-5781

Blue Chip Casino Hotel
777 Blue Chip Dr
Michigan City, IN
219-879-7711

Comfort Inn
1915 Mississippi St
Merrillville, IN
219-947-7677

Econo Lodge
6201 Opportunity Ln
Merrillville, IN
815-259-7378

Bike Shops

My Bike of Michigan City
1801 Franklin St
Michigan City, IN
219-879-0899

Chesterton Bicycle Station
116 S 4th St
Chesterton, IN
219-926-1112

Dick's Sporting Goods
2255 Southlake Mall
Merrillville, IN
219-791-0610

New Buffalo to Oak Ridge Prairie Park (44 miles)

Miles N/S	Directions	Dist	R	Service	Miles S/N
0	R at SL on US12 (*New Buffalo)	2.9	3	CGLQR	44
3	R on Unsigned then L on Grand Beach Rd	0.2	2		41
3	R at SS on Royal Ave	0.2	2		41
3	S at SS on Station Rd	0.6	2		41
4	R at SS on Dogwood Dr	0.2	2		40
4	L at SS pm Ridgeview Dr	0.4	2		40
5	R at SS on Tahoma Tr	0.1	3		39
5	L at SS on Lake Shore Dr	5.5	2		39
10	L on Franklin St (*Michigan City)	0.3	3	CGLQR	34
10	VR on 2nd St	0.1	3		33
11	L on Wabash St	0.1	3		33
11	R at SS on Michigan Blvd/US 12	1.6	4		33
12	VR on Beverly Dr	2.1	3		32
14	R on Lake Shore Cty Rd	0.4	2		30
15	L at SS Lake Front Dr	2.2	2	C	29
17	L on E State Park Rd	1.2	2		27
18	R on Calumet Tr (gravel)	2.9	1		26
21	*Dune Park train station/Indiana Dunes SP	0.0		C	23
21	S on Calumet Trail (gravel)	0.2	1		23
21	L on Waverly Rd	2.0	3	Q	23
23	R at SS on Woodlawn Ave	0.2	3		21
23	L at SS on 15th St (*Chesterton)	0.3	3	R	20
24	R on Praire Duneland Tr	11.0	P		20
35	L on Hobart Rd then R at SL on Cleveland Ave/SH 51 (*Hobart)	0.1	3		9
35	L on Liberty St	0.1	3		9
35	R on Devonshire St	0.2	3		9
35	L at SS on Indiana St then R on Lillian St then L on Illinois St	0.2	3		9
35	L on Georgianna St	0.1	3		9
35	R on Indiana St	0.3	3		8
36	R at SS on 6th St/Linda St	0.1	3		8
36	R on Oak Savannah Tr (OST)	3.1	P		8
39	S on OST across Liverpool Rd	4.3	P		5
43	L to cross Main St cont OST	0.6	P		1
44	R to exit Oak Ridge Prairie Park parking		1		0

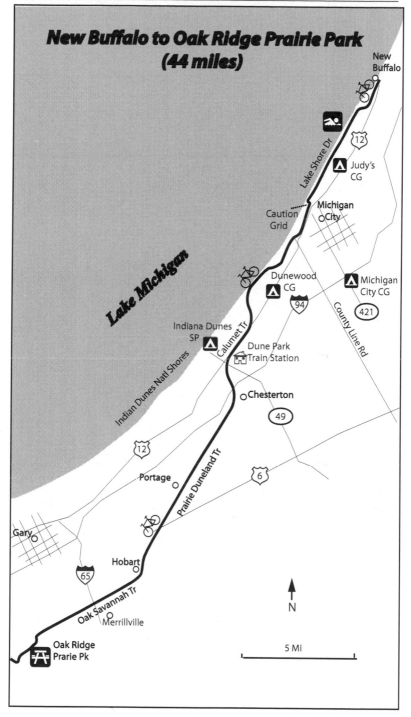

New Buffalo to Oak Ridge Prairie Park (44 miles)

Lake Michigan Trail
SECTION 2

Oak Ridge Prairie Park to Edgewater (44 miles)

When researching the route along Indiana's Lake Michigan shoreline I was fortunate to find Nancy Tibbett, Executive Director of Bicycle Indiana IndyBike Hub/YMCA. She told me about the bicycle friendly routes documented by the Northwest Indiana Regional Planning Committee. A lot of the routes were on separated bike trails built on abandoned railways that I was not aware existed.

I later discovered that I wasn't the only one who had not heard about the bike paths. On my ride through this area, after exiting the Oak Savannah Trail I met a cyclist coming from Seattle enroute to New York City who didn't know about the bike paths either. I turned around to escort him over the Oak Savannah Trail then stayed with him to the trailhead of the Duneland Trail. He was very appreciative and said it made for a much more enjoyable ride through the area than he had anticipated.

While riding the Erie Lakawanna Trail (ELT) be sure to take time to read the markers documenting the history of the area. Also, as the route overlaps Broad Street, you can continue straight to enter the town of Griffith for a lunch break. If you would like to log more miles before a break, there are several opportunities to find places to eat near many of the street crossings along the trail.

It is easy to miss the approach to the Kennedy Avenue crossing on the ELT. There is a trail that continues straight but we take the fork to the left to reach the crossing. Watch for a large abstract polished metal art piece at the junction of the turn. The art structure is dedicated to the spirit of the Highland community's downtown renovation. Also check out the huge mural painted on the wall of the overpass at the crossing. Highland has some very talented artists in the area.

Another turn to watch for on the ELT is the one for Eaton Street. The ELT does not cross the street, instead Eaton T-bones the trail from the right. Just match the distance on the Mileage Log to the turn and you shouldn't have any problem identifying it.

As you veer left on 130th Street on your approach to the

William W. Powers State Fish & Wildlife Area, the entrance on Alternate Avenue O isn't actually a street. It is an entrance to the park maintenance facility, however, it is the best route to enter the park. If the gate is closed just continue straight to Avenue O, and then take a right to reach one of the other entrances into the park.

Stop to check out the Nike missile mounted in the park. It is one ominous looking weapon. It isn't every day you have an opportunity to get an up-close and personal inspection of one.

The Burnham Greenway Trail (BGT) is another abandoned railway that routes you through residential neighborhoods. This area has done a nice job utilizing these old right-of-ways as a means of transportation to get around. But even though there are a lot of abandoned railways in this area, they still have a very active railway system. Some of the trains are pretty long, too. I had to wait several minutes for a train to pass at one crossing, and just as the end of the train was in sight, another train came from the opposite direction that I had to wait for, too. You should also use caution when approaching railroad crossings on the BGT, some of them are pretty rough.

As you approach the overpass at the end of Ewing Avenue, and you duck under the overpass leading to 100th Street, again use caution. This is a blind corner for automobiles. I rode on the sidewalk while under the overpass. After emerging from the overpass you can drop back on the street to enter Calumet Park.

You may have noticed some of the route you've been riding on has been signed as the Lake Front Trail Connection. This is in reference to the Lake Front Trail (LFT) that borders Lake Michigan in Chicago. LFT is a true jewel for cyclists and you don't have much further to go to reach it.

Just after crossing the Calumet River Bridge you will pass the Lake Shore Drive Extension on your right. On my tour through the area this highway was still under construction. I rode on it as far as I was allowed and didn't see any signs of it including a bike path. But you might want to check it out yourself when you come through. If they have added one hopefully it will connect to the LFT. (If there is a bike path, please send me an email and let me know where it takes you.)

When you reach the end of Shore Drive, continue across 71st Street to begin riding the LFT. Initially it isn't much more than a sidewalk, but it quickly develops into a full-blown separated bike path. Once you reach the path sit back in your saddle and relax, because the LFT is a model for how other cities should develop their waterfront shores.

Most of the LFT routes cyclists right along the lakeshore, and there are also a variety of interesting sites to check out. You will ride beside legendary Soldier Field, home of "Da Bears". Next to this is the state-of-the-art Field Museum. And just after crossing the Chicago River you pass an amusement park. You might want to schedule a break just past the Navy Pier to watch some really awesome beach volleyball. Chicago's History Museum is also alongside the LFT, plus countless other places to visit. This would be a great place to setup a home base at one of the hotels listed in the guide and spend a few days exploring the area.

You will also pass several places to grab a snack at some of the beach eateries, such as Dock Street Café (on the Navy Pier), and Oak Street Beach Food & Drink a little further north. There are other places also that you will see signs for.

If you do decide to spend some time in the area you can pick up tourist information at the Visitor Center, located at 163 East Pearson Street. To reach the center, turn left off the LFT on East Chicago Avenue, then ride a couple blocks and turn right on North Michigan Avenue for another block. There is also internet access at the Public Library which is also located here.

My favorite stop along the LFT is "The Bean" at Millennium Park. Its real name is Cloud Gate, but the huge chrome sculpture is better known by its nickname because of its bean-like shape. During my visit I slowly circled the entire sculpture to view the every changing reflection of Chicago's downtown skyline. In the photo in the guide you can see my reflection from behind in The Bean. A lot of people were having fun with this by taking pictures of themselves taking their picture.

You can reach the park by exiting the LFT on East Monroe Street. Follow this street for a couple of blocks and the park will be on your right.

If you are flying into Chicago to begin your Lake Michigan Adventure, Demian, at Lakeshore Bike, said you can ship your bike to his shop. If it requires assembly or a tune up before heading out his full service shop has everything required to get it ready. Give him a call and he will also help you plot your train route to his shop from the airport.

After 18 miles of fantastic cycling, the LFT curves around to lead you onto Ardmore Avenue. You are on this for less than a block before reaching Sheridan Avenue, and the end of Section 2.

Having fun at The Bean in Millennium Park.

Camping (note: watch for proposed camping on Chicago's Northerly Island)
N/A

Lodging

Inn of Hammond
7813 Indianapolis Ave
Hammond, IN
219-845-4678

Swissotel
323 W Wacker Dr
Chicago, IL
312-565-0565

Hyde Park Arms Hotel
5316 S Harper Ave
Chicago, IL
773-493-3500

Flemish House B&B
68 E Cedar St
Chicago, IL
312-664-9981

The Wheller Mansion
2020 S Calumet Ave
Chicago, IL
312-945-2020

Best Western Hotel
3434 N Broadway St
Chicago, IL
773-244-3434

Bike Shops

Lakeshore Bike
3650 N Recreation Dr
Chicago, IL
773-348-7668

Blackstone Bike
6100 S Blackston
Chicago, IL
773-241-5458

On the Route Bicycles
1118 S Michigan Ave
Chicago, IL
312-588-1050

Bicycle Clinic
2221 E 71st Street
Chicago, IL
773-955-2028

DJ's Bike Doctor
1500 E 55th St
Chicago, IL
773-955-4400

Goodspeed Cycles
754 Burnham Ave
Calumet City, IL
708-891-2600

Oak Ridge Prairie Park to Edgewater (44 Miles)

Miles N/S	Directions	Dist	R	Service	Miles S/N
0	R to exit Oak Ridge Prairie Park parking	1.1	1		44
1	L at SS on Colfax St/Arbogsat Ave	0.7	3		43
2	R on Erie Lakawanna Tr (ELT)	0.8	P		42
3	L on Ave B then R on Broad St	0.2	L		41
3	L on ELT (*Griffith)	3.0	P	QR	41
6	VL to cross Kennedy Ave cont on ELT	0.7	P		38
7	L at SS on Grand Blvd (*Highland)	0.1	2		37
7	VL at Sycamore Ave to cont on ELT thru tunnel	0.2	P		37
7	R at intersection after exiting tunnel	0.4	P		37
7	R on trail to cross Little Calumet River	0.1	P		37
7	L to cont on ELT	0.6	P	QR	37
8	VR to cont on ELT around Cabela store	3.5	p		36
11	R on Eaton St then L on Sohl Ave/Johnson Ave	2.6	3		33
14	L at SS on 138th St	0.2	3		30
14	R on Hoffman Ave/Sheffield Ave	0.2	4	Q	30
14	L on 136th St/134th St	1.2	4		30
16	R on Ave N	0.5	3		28
16	VL on 130th St	0.1	3		28
16	R on Alt Ave O (unsigned)	0.1	1		28
16	L at YS on Wolf Lake Blvd	1.2	1		28
18	L on Burnham Greenway Tr (BGT) then R at intersection	2.4	P		26
20	Cross Ewing Ave/US 12 to cont BGT	0.6	P	R	24
21	R under overpass Ewing Ave/E 100th St	0.3	L		23
21	Follow S Crilly Dr/98th St/Walton Dr/Foreman Dr around Calumet Park	1.5	1		23
22	R on 95th St to exit park	0.2	2		22
23	R on Ewing Ave/Mackinaw Ave/US 41	1.0	3	R	21
24	L on 87th St/US 41	0.1	3		20
24	R at SL on Burley Ave/US 41	0.3	3		20
24	L at SS on 85th St/Baker St/US 41	0.1	3		20
24	R on Bond St/Shore Dr/US 41	1.9	L		20
26	S on Lake Front Trail (*Chicago)	18.0	P		18
44	S on Ardmore Ave	0.0			0
44	R on Sheridan Ave (*Edgewater)		4		0

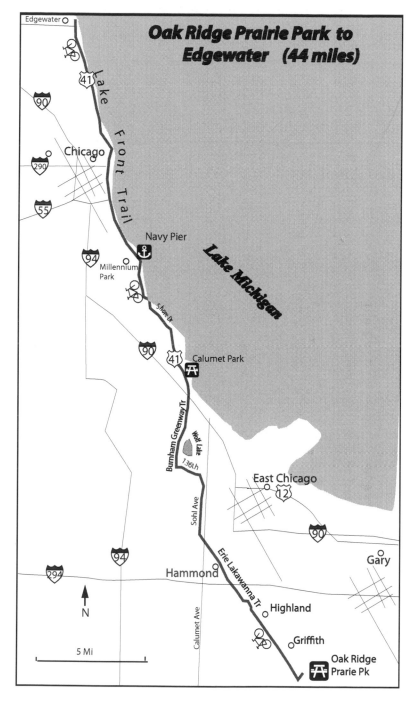

Oak Ridge Prairie Park to Edgewater (44 miles)

Lake Michigan Trail
SECTION 3

Edgewater to Kenosha (59 miles)

At the turn off Sheridan Avenue you not only enter another street, you enter another world. The ride along Devon Avenue takes cyclists on a tour through Indian, Pakistani, Russian, Bangladeshi, and a whole gumbo of other international neighborhoods that is collectively known as "Little India." If you enjoy eating authentic ethnic foods be sure to schedule your lunch or dinner for when you are riding this street. With the global mix of restaurants and markets to choose from you will be glad you did.

Devon Avenue is a busy, crowded, congested street, filled with people dressed in the colorful interesting costumes from their homelands. Initially there is a painted bike lane, but shortly after the first mile it disappears and you are forced to blend in with the hordes of automobiles, delivery trucks, pedestrians, and people riding bicycles in street clothes.

The traffic can get pretty heavy on Devon, but with street lights on each block and a steady stream of pedestrians crossing the road wherever they feel like it, at least you don't have to worry about speeding motorists. Just sit back and enjoy the cosmopolitan atmosphere. Neighborhoods like Little India that make touring large cities interesting.

If you prefer to avoid Devon Avenue you can remain on Sheridan Avenue all the way to Kenosha, the end of this section. But Sheridan Avenue is a pretty busy highway, and motorists are driving high speeds. Trade-offs, that's what life is all about.

If you need a bike shop, turn left off Devon Avenue onto North Clark Street to find Gary's Cycle Shop, listed in the guide. If you are looking for a true bohemian experience, stop off at The Hookah Joint, 2755 West Devon Avenue. A girl told me it's sexier than cigarettes

After a little over three miles the traffic congestion lessons as Devon Avenue widens to four lanes. However, the speed picks up.

The entrance to the North Branch Trail (NBT) is on the right, just after crossing Caldwell Avenue. It ducks in amongst dense mature trees of a forest preserve. The NBT weaves through various neighborhood parks, many with restrooms and water, and crosses several busy streets as it snakes its way alongside the North Branch Chicago River. Follow the trails marked with a red blaze until reaching the turn into the Botanic Gardens.

The Holiday Inn listed in the guide is located less than two miles east on Touhy Avenue. At the Dumpster Street crossing, you can ride west less than a half mile to reach a Dominick's Food Center and Starbucks, or a half mile to the east to reach Giordanos, what many Chicagoans claim is home of "Chicago's Best Pizza". As always, when you patronize an establishment be sure to let them know that you are on a bicycle. If people see cyclists as a potential customer rather than an obstacle in the road maybe they will be more acceptable to bicycles on the highways.

Don't be surprised if you encounter horses on the NBT. There is an equestrian center located alongside the trail at the Golf Road crossing. After crossing Golf Road there is a trail leading off to the right. We will stay left, continuing to follow the red blazed route.

There are several routes you can follow through the twenty-six gardens and four natural areas within the Chicago Botanic Garden. One of the site's more renowned attractions is the Bonsai Collection. There are numerous opportunities to pause alongside three miles of extended shoreline for a relaxing rest or lunch break. At the top of each hour the air throughout the garden area is filled with the melodious chimes of the 95-foot-tall bell tower, which looms high over the lush forest of trees. If the timing is right, maybe your visit will coincide with one of the regularly scheduled carillon concerts.

When you are ready to leave the gardens, use the Lake Cook exit, or else you could find yourself cycling in a perpetual loop, like I did, before finding the correct route out of the garden.

The entrance for the Skokie Valley Trail (SVT) is located behind the convenience store at the corner of Lake Cook Road and Skokie Boulevard. The Courtyard Chicago Highland Hotel listed in the guide is located one block further west of the entrance to the SVT.

The people of this area really take advantage of this green space by locating the railway, a utility right-of-way, and the bike path on a common strip of land. The corporate sponsorship for the trail cleverly labeled it a "rail-with-trail." It's great to see the business community get behind bike trails.

If you are in need of bike repairs, or just want to visit with fellow cyclists, the Trek Bicycle Shop is located in the shopping center on the right of Park Avenue just after leaving the SVT.

The entrance to the Robert McClory Bike Trail (RMBT) is another easy to miss entry. As you are riding along Vine Avenue, the trail is located to the left of the entrance for the Highland Park High School parking lot. I hope the students take advantage of the convenience of having a bike trail running by the school. The RMBT is known by many different names over the route, and it's confusing trying to determine when one stops and the next begins, so just follow the descriptions in the Mileage Log and it won't matter what name a particular section has been given.

An interesting site to visit near the RMBT is the Fort Sheridan Historic Cemetery. Generations of American military service members have been buried at the cemetery since its creation in 1889. It is interesting to stroll across these well maintained grounds to read headstones of veterans from as far back as the Civil War. To reach the cemetery continue riding on Sheridan Avenue past the train station north of Highwood, where the RMBT resumes once again, and after another half-a-mile you will pass the entrance on your right.

As I rode through the parking lot for the train station in Lake Forest it was great to see the lot filled with vehicles of people taking advantage of the mass transit system.

Lake Forest is a quaint village with a picturesque town square. It is a great setting to pause for a cup of coffee or tea before continuing on your tour.

If you enjoy art, be sure to stop at the Station Art Gallery in Lake Bluff. The gallery is located in the old train station and the RMBT runs right past the entrance. You will probably have an opportunity to visit with the artists of the work on display because the gallery is ran and staffed by the exhibiting artists.

The intersection for the 24th Street turn is located just past the entrance to the Great Lakes Naval Station. At the stop light, turn right and circle around under the overpass you just crossed over to reach Commonwealth Avenue.

After crossing Martin Luther King Boulevard you resume RMBT. The next twelve miles of the RMBT has a crushed stone surface. It makes for a nice ride if you are equipped with the proper tires, but I wouldn't recommend riding it with tires narrower than 25 millimeter tires. If you prefer to avoid this part of the RMBT you can turn right on any east bound street to reach Sheridan Road/ State Highway 32 and rejoin the guide in Kenosha.

If you remain on the RMBT, other than sections of the route within the residential neighborhoods of Waukegan and Zion, you are riding through farm country with a tree lined buffer separating the trail from the cultivated fields. For services you will have to exit the trail. A couple of the more useful exits will be to turn left on Grand Avenue in Waukegan and right on 29th Street to reach downtown Zion. For the bicycle shop in Waukegan turn left off RMBT on Grand Avenue and ride about a half mile.

The only camping in this section is the Illinois Beach State Park in Zion. There are two separate sections of the park, referred to as "north" and "south" park. Only the south park offers camping. The south park also encompasses the only remaining beach ridge shoreline in Illinois. Both parks are known for their bird watching opportunities and possess some of the larger sand dunes in the area.

When the path surface transitions to pavement you have reached the Kenosha County Bike Trail (KCBT). After you begin riding the KCBT, once you ride the bridge over County Road A1, say goodbye to Illinois and give a big hello to Wisconsin.

Kenosha has established what it calls a Pike Bike Trail (PBT), which is a combination of bike friendly streets and separated paved paths to route you through the city. Most of the turns for the route are signed but some are not, so follow the Mileage Log and don't rely totally on the route signs.

The PBT makes for a pleasant ride as it routes cyclists past the type of attractions I generally look for in a city such as parks, beach areas, museums, and historic sites. If you would like to learn more about what the area offers, visit the Visitor Information Center, located at 812 56th Street to find more detailed materials. For those who skip the Visitor Center, you will find many of the attractions in the Kenosha Harbor area.

The Kenosha Lakeshore Path terminates at the base of the 50th Street Bridge. You can either carry your bike up the steps beside the bridge or you can push it up a social trail to the left of the steps. When you reach the bridge, if you are still looking for a place to eat or an adult beverage, turn right on 7th Avenue for a block to the Boat House Pub & Eatery. To reach the Best Western listed in the guide, turn left on 7th Avenue. You will also find the Ski & Sport Chalet bike shop in that same area.

Camping

Illinois Beach SP
Lake Front Dr
Zion, IL
847-662-4811

Lodging

Holiday Inn
5300 W Touhy Ave
Skokie, IL
800-315-2621

*Courtyard Chicago Highland
1505 Lake Cook Rd
Highland Park, IL
847-831-3338

The Deer Path Inn
225 E Illinois Road,
Lake Forest, IL
847-234-2280

Sunset Motel
511 Rockland Rd
Lake Bluff, IL
847-234-4669

Robert's Roost Motel
1705 N Sheridan Rd
Waukegan, IL
847-623-7200

Illinois Beach Resort
1 Lake Front Dr
Zion, IL
847-625-7300

Sun Inn Motel
301 Sheridan Rd
Winthrop Harbor, IL
847-746-7380

Best Western Inn
5125 6th Ave
Kenosha, IL
262-658-3281

Southport B & B
4404 7th Ave
Kenosha, WI
262-652-1951

Bike Shops

Gary's Cycle Shop
6317 N Clark St
Chicago, IL
773-743-4201

Midwest Bicycle & Billards
1928 Grand Ave
Waukegan, IL
847-249-5670

Ski & Sport Chalet
5039 6th Ave
Kenosha, WI
262-658-8515

Edgewater to Kenosha (59 miles)

Miles N/S	Directions	Dist	R	Service	Miles S/N
0	R on Sheridan Ave	0.9	4		59
1	R on Devon Ave	5.4	4	R	58
6	R on North Branch Trail (NBT)	1.2	P		53
8	L on Touhy Ave to cross a bridge then R on NBT	2.5	P		52
10	Cross Dempster St at SL then R to follow bike arrows	0.2	P		49
10	L on NBT (*Morton Grove)	1.8	P		49
12	VL after crossing Golf Rd	4.4	P		47
16	At SL crossing Willow Rd to cont on NBT	1.7	P		43
18	L to cross Tower Rd	2.2			41
20	VR to Parallel Dundee Rd then L on blue marked trail to cross Dundee Rd to Chicago	1.0			39
21	R to exit Gardens	0.2			38
22	L at SL on County Line Rd/Lake Cook Rd	0.9	4		38
22	R on Skokie Valley Trail after crossing Skokie Valley Rd	2.8	P	Q	37
25	R on Park Ave	1.0	3	R	34
26	*Highland Park			R	33
26	L on Midlothian Ave	0.2	2		33
26	R on Vine Ave	0.2	2		33
27	L on Robert McClory Bike Trail (RMBT)	0.6	P		33
27	L after crossing Waukegan Ave then R on Bloom St	0.2	2		32
27	L on St Johns Ave	0.4	L		32
28	L at SS on Walker Ave	0.1	P		31
28	R on Lakeview Ave/Clay Ave	0.4	P		31
28	*Highwood			GLQR	31
28	R on Sheridan Rd/Waukegan Ave	1.0	P	QLR	31
29	L to cross Sheridan Ave then R on RMBT	2.4	P		30
32	Ride thru train station parking lot to cont on RMBT (*Lake Forest)	2.1	2	GLQR	28
34	*Lake Bluff	2.5	P	GLQR	25
36	R at SL 24th St to cross Sheridan Rd and follow trail under overpass	0.5	P		23
37	R on Commonwealth Ave	0.2	P		22
37	R after crossing MLK Blvd the L on RMBT	0.3	P		22
37	*North Chicago			GLQR	22

37	RMBT becomes crushed stone	2.7	P		22
40	*Waukegan			GLQR	19
40	S on RMBT	5.8			19
46	*Zion			CGLQR	13
46	S on RMBT	3.5			13
49	S on Kenosha County Milti-use Trail	3.5	P		10
53	R on 89th St	0.7	2		6
54	R on 17th Ave	0.2	2		6
54	L on 91st St	0.6	2		6
54	VL on7th Ave	1.4	2		5
56	R on 78th St	0.2	2		4
56	VR on Southport Park Path	0.5	P		3
56	VR on 1st Ave	0.2	2		3
57	L on 71st St then R at YS on 2nd Ave	0.1	2		3
57	L on 69th St then R on 3rd Ave	0.7	2		3
57	R on Kenosha Lakeshore Path	1.8	P		2
59	R on 50th St to cross bridge (*Kenosha)		2		0

Happy cyclist enjoying the Robert McClory Bike Trail.

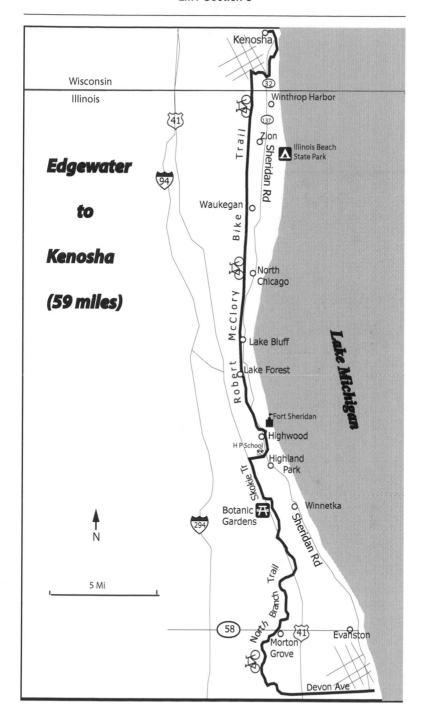

Edgewater

to

Kenosha

(59 miles)

Lake Michigan Trail
SECTION 4

Kenosha to Glendale (52 miles)

The Pike Bike Path (PBP) is to your left after riding across the 50th Street Bridge. If you have time for a short detour there are some interesting sites to visit within a half a mile ride off the route. Just continue straight on 50th Street and then curve around 4th Avenue to reach the Kenosha History Center, Simmons Island Beach, Southport Lighthouse Museum, and the North Pierhead Lighthouse.

If you're like me and are wondering where the name of the bike path came from, in Native American dialect Kenosha means Pike, so Kenosha Bike Path.

Much of the PBP routes cyclists through parks and along the shoreline, with excellent views of Lake Michigan. It ends at the entrance to Carthage College. You will then ride another designated bike friendly street connection route that will lead you through several Kenosha neighborhoods to reach the County Line Bike Path (CLBP). The CLBP is another piece of the Milwaukee-Racine-Kenosha (MRK) trail system. This section of abandoned rail right-of-away that takes you through the heartland of farm country.

Shortly after the path crosses Chicory Road, the CLBP will continue straight, but you will turn right on Concord Drive. This is the beginning of the South Racine Street Connection. This biker friendly route weaves through neighborhoods on quiet, low traffic side streets all the way to downtown Racine.

The Lake Michigan Pathway (LMP) hugs the wharf in Racine to give cyclists an opportunity to view the boat activities in the busy harbor. There are historic markers along the route and a food concession. It's somewhat confusing when the LMP appears to dead end at 4th Street. Just zag to your left and you will immediately see where the LMP continues on across the street.

Upon reaching Main Street you can take a short ride to the left for a tour of historic downtown Racine, where you will have a choice of several nice restaurants to eat. When you are ready to continue your tour, as you ride Main Street over the Root River Bridge I recommend using the sidewalk to avoid the metal grill of the bridge. Once across the bridge there are still more opportunities for food and drink at a couple of bar & grills you pass along the river bank on Dodge Street.

Once the LMB pulls away from the harbor area it continues alongside North Beach Park with more interesting historic markers, a visitor information center, the Racine Zoological Gardens, plus an optional short side trip to the Reef Point Beacon.

The MRK trail surface in this next area is crushed stone. You can avoid the segment by riding Douglas Road, which parallels the trail all the way to 6 Mile Road. However, I recommend riding the trail because Douglas Road is pretty busy and there isn't much of a shoulder. The crushed stone in this area is pretty packed, so it should be alright for most bicycles.

After riding on a several busy highways the tranquil setting of the Oak Leaf Trail (OLT) is a welcome experience. It's great that the area leaders have preserved this long greenway for the enjoyment of the masses rather than chopping it up into private housing lots for the pleasure of a select few.

Riding along the tall bluffs that border the trail, with vast views across the lake, I am reminded of touring Highway 101 on the California coast. Lake Michigan is too wide to see the opposite bank and has waves lapping the shoreline, so it is a lot like an ocean.

As you near the end of this section of the OLT, pause to enjoy the view of the Milwaukee skyline. At this point the OLT ends at the South Shore Marina parking lot. There are public restrooms conveniently located in the lot. While riding Russell Avenue after crossing the parking area, you pass a neighborhood bar and deli. This is a good place to take a break before entering Milwaukee.

As with most large cities, hotels are pretty expensive in the downtown Milwaukee area. But if you want to stay in the hub of the city there are several hotels to choose from. The Hotel Metro listed in the guide has an interesting history to go along with being centrally located.

If you would like more information about sites to visit in the area, stop at the visitor center located at 400 West Virginia, or call them at 414-908-6001. You can also learn more about the Lake Express Ferry to Muskegon, Michigan.

For a nice side trip, take a left when you reach Ellis Street to investigate the interesting sites within the Historic Third Ward District, which include the Riverwalk along the Milwaukee River, the Public Market, and with many others. The Milwaukee community has done a great job of preserving these unique old buildings and created an exciting atmosphere for the downtown district itself.

After your tour of the historic area and you have returned to Ellis Street, continue your ride alongside the river under the impressive Hoan Bridge, and then circle around the Marcus Amphitheatre to reach the beginning of the Hank Aaron State Trail. There are several forks in the trail as it meanders along the lakeshore. There is no need for concern about getting lost; the trails will all merge together before the next turn listed in the Mileage Log.

If you enjoy science you might want to stop at Discovery World. It is geared towards young people, but the aquarium alone makes it worth a visit. The trail passes right by so it makes for a nice break from your ride. You will also pass the Milwaukee Art Museum. Even if you don't go in the museum be sure to stop and admire the amazing sail boat shaped building housing the museum.

After crossing Lincoln Memorial Drive the first part of this section of the OLT isn't much more than a wide sidewalk, so be courteous to pedestrians. Soon it opens up enough that some of the locals have even cultivated a string of bountiful vegetable gardens along the shoulders of the trail.

Shortly after crossing Capital Drive in Shorewood watch for a branch of the OLT that turns to the left, leading to Estabrook Park. If you are just riding along enjoying the sights it is easy to miss the turn and continue straight.

There is heavy traffic at the Hampton Road crossing, so use caution. Immediately after crossing Hampton Road you turn left again to cross busy Port Washington Road. Once across this intersection you will veer off to the right on the next section of the OLT, which runs through a linear park along the Milwaukee River. After the Bender Road crossing, pause to enjoy the nice waterfall on your right.

If you are planning to spend the night in Glendale turn right off Milwaukee River Parkway onto Silver Spring Drive. After riding less than a mile you will then turn right on Port Washington Road to reach the motels listed in the guidebook.

One more turn to watch for as you finish up Section 4 is when you reach Green Tree Road. There is a bike sign directing you to turn right, but we are following the beat of a different drum and will continue straight.

Camping

Yogi Bear's Jellystone Park
8425 State Road 38
Caledonia, WI
262-835-2565

Lodging

Beach Aire Motel
1147 Sheridan Rd
Kenosha, WI
262-552-8131

*Radisson Hotel Racine
223 Gas Light Cir
Racine, WI
262-632-7777

Howard Johnson
700 W Virginia St
Milwaukee, WI
414-276-4546

Seeker Motel
1700 Durand Ave
Racine, WI
262-637-8555

*Victoria Motel
10131 S Chicago Rd
Oak Creek. WI
414-762-6062

Baymont Inn
5485 N Port Washington Rd
Glendale, WI
414-961-7272

Locknaiar Inn B&B
1121 Lake Ave
Racine, WI
262-633-3300
(near entry to LMP)

Hotel Metro
411 E Masson St
Milwaukee, WI
414-223-1158

La Quinta Inn
5110 N Port Washington Rd
Glendale, WI
414-962-6767

Bike Shops

Total Cyclery
2900 52nd St
Kenosha, WE
262-652-2222

South Shore Cyclery
4758 S Packard Ave
Cudahy, WI
414-831-0211

Racine Cyclery & Fitness
4615 Washington Ave (SH 20)
Racine, WI
262-637-7241

Crank Daddy's
2170 N Prospect
Milwaukee, WI
414-347-5511

3rd Coast Bicycles
210 3rd St
Racine, WI
262-634-0484

Rainbow Jersey
4600 N Wilson Dr
Shorewood, WI
414-961-1110

Impressive view of Milwaukee skyline!

Kenosha to Glendale (52 miles)

Miles N/S	Directions	Dist	R	Service	Miles S/N
0	R on 50th St to cross bridge (*Kenosha)	0.1	2		52
0	L on Pike Bike Path (PBP)	2.9	P		52
3	VL at SL to cross Alford Park Dr/SH 32 then parallel Sheridan Rd	0.2	P		49
3	R to cross Sheridan Rd to parallel Birch Rd	0.2	P		49
3	R on 15th Ave	0.5	2		49
4	L on 15th St	0.4	2		48
4	R on PBP parallel 20th Ave	0.5	P		48
5	S across 12th St to County Line Bike Path (CLBP)	3.3	P		47
8	R on Concord Dr	0.1	3		44
8	L on Knoll Pl	0.6	3		44
9	R on Maryland Ave for 1 blk	0.0	3		43
9	L on Drexel Ave	0.7	3	QR	43
10	R on Gilson St	0.3	3		43
10	L at SS on James Blvd	0.2	3		42
10	S at SS on Case Ave	0.3	3		42
10	R at SS on De Koven Ave	1.0	3		42
11	L on Wisconsin Ave	0.3	3		41
12	R at SS on 16th St 1 blk	0.0	3		41
12	*Racine			GLQR	41
12	L on Main St	0.6	3		41
12	R on 11th St	0.1	3		40
12	R on Lake Michigan Pathway (LMP)	0.9	P		40
13	L on 4th St then R on LMP	0.6	P		39
14	R on Main St	0.1	3		38
14	R on Dodge St	0.1	3	R	38
14	L on Michigan Blvd then R on Reichert Ct	0.2	2		38
14	L on LMP	1.4	P		38
16	S on Michigan Blvd	0.1	4		37
16	L on Melvon Ave	0.3	3		37
16	R at SS on Erie St	0.2	3		36
16	L on South St	1.0	3		36
17	R on Milwaukee-Racine-Kenosha (MRK) (crushed stone)	2.4	P		35
20	L Douglas Ave then R to cont on MRK	1.6	P		33
21	L on 6 Mile Rd	1.3	3		31

23	R on Botting Rd	1.7	3		30
24	Cross SH 32 then L on WE Energies Tr (crushed stone)	0.9	P		28
25	L on Elm Rd then R on Chicago Ave/SH 32	2.5	4	QR	27
28	*Oak Creek			GLQR	25
28	S on Chicago Ave/SH 32	1.5		QR	25
29	R at SS to cont on SH 32/Marquette Ave	0.2	4		23
29	*South Milwaukee			GLQR	23
29	L at SL to cont on SH 32/10th Ave/N Chicago Ave	0.6	3		23
30	R on Oak Creek Pkwy	1.3	2		22
31	R on Oak Leaf Tr (OLT)	7.7	P		21
39	S across South Shore Marina parking lot to cont on trail	0.3	1		13
39	S on Russel Ave	0.3	3	GR	13
40	R on Bay St (*Milwaukee)	1.0	2	Q	13
41	R on Kinnickinnic Ave/SH 32	0.5	5		12
41	R on 1st St/SH32	1.0	5	QR	11
42	R at SL on Pittsburg Ave/SH 32	0.2	5		10
42	R at SL on Erie St/SH 32	0.6	2		10
43	S on Hank Aaron State Tr	1.2	P		9
44	L on Art Museum Dr to cross Lincolin Memorial Dr	0.0	3		8
44	R on Oak Leaf Tr (OLT)	3.1	P		8
47	L on OLT shortly after crossing Capitol Dr (*Shorewood)	1.5	P		5
49	R at SL to cross Hampton Rd then L to cross Port Washington Rd	0.0	P		4
49	S on OLT thru golf course parking area.	0.6	P		4
49	S after crossing bridge to cont on OLT	0.1	P		3
49	S to continue on OLT at fork	1.0	P		3
50	S on Milwaukee River Pkwy	1.0	2		2
51	S to cross Bender Rd to cont on OLT	0.9	P		1
52	S to cross Green Tree Rd to cont on OLT (*Glendale)		P		0

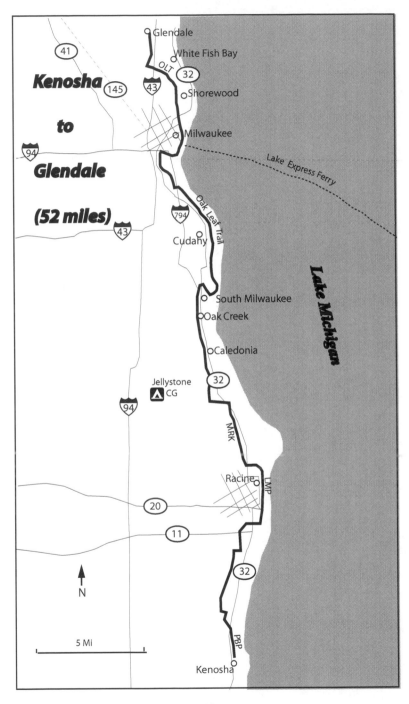

Lake Michigan Trail
SECTION 5

Glendale to Sheboygan (53 miles)

As a result of the limited available highways along the shores of Lake Michigan in this area, most of the LMT for this section of Wisconsin takes you inland. There are several short stretches of highways that are closer to the lake; however, these leave major gaps when you try to link them to create a continuous bicycle friendly route. Even the Lake Michigan Circle Tour for automobiles was forced to use Interstate 43 through here. So, the guidebook will follow a bicycle friendly route established by Wisconsin Coastal Guide that utilizes numerous separated paved bike paths. As it turns out this makes for a great ride through the beautiful farm country and quaint villages.

Speaking of separated bike paths, shortly after beginning this section you pick up the Brown Deer Trail (BDT) out of Brown Deer Park. The start of the trail is on your right just after passing the park exit. If you happen to have brought a golf disc along, the park offers a challenging course. A round of disc golf is a good way to get off your bike to stretch your legs.

Plan your schedule to stop for a lunch or dinner break at Spanky's Hideway, located at the West County Line Road crossing. It is right alongside the trail on the left. This is a nice neighborhood bar & grill where the workers and patrons are a friendly bunch who treat you like a regular. This crossing is also where you begin riding the Ozaukee Interurban Trail (OIT).

The OIT was built on the right-of-way that was once used for the rapid transit electric railway system established in 1905, linking Milwaukee with the surrounding communities.

If you are running low on ramen noodles or any other food essentials, there is a Piggly Wiggly on the right at the Mequon Road crossing. I mention this because sometimes it's difficult to find a grocery store from a trail and this one is really conveniently located. There are also several restaurants at the crossing.

Cedarburg is a nice picturesque village that is ideal for sight-seeing from the seat of a bicycle. The downtown streets are lined with well-preserved historic buildings that are now occupied by interesting shops and art galleries. There are also a variety of businesses where you can take a break to treat yourself to a snack and do a little people watching. Many of the beautiful buildings you will see are the original structures from the 1840s, when the town was founded by German and Irish immigrants. Washington Avenue is the best street to start your tour. The visitor information center is located at W61 N480 Washington Avenue for materials to help you explore this historic town. You can also get directions at the center for a short side trip to see the last remaining covered bridge in Wisconsin.

As you ride through the Grafton, Wisconsin of today, it is difficult to believe that this community was once the home for one of the most influential Blues recording companies in the country. In the 1920s the town's Paramount Records was "the place" for Blues musicians to go to record their music. The Wisconsin Chair Company, in nearby Port Washington, started the recording company to encourage people to buy more of the phonographs they manufactured. It's an interesting story. Stop by the Grafton Public Library to pick up a self-guided Paramount Walking Tour brochure to experience firsthand this important chapter in the Blues music industry. Following your visit, as you ride along the OIT, try to visualize Blind Lemon Jefferson, Charlie Patton, and other famous Blues musicians of the era traveling this same right-of-way in the mass transit electric railway system of that period.

After leaving Grafton, as the OIT crosses Interstate 43 the overpass provides cyclists with a rare elevated view. This is a good spot to stop to admire the scenery. With the exception of a few views off a bluff along Lake Michigan there aren't many opportunities like this, so be sure to take advantage of it.

On the approach entering Port Washington along Park Street you pass a Union Cemetery that was founded in 1854. There are some interesting headstones within this historic site and the writings on several of the markers are in a foreign language, demonstrating the European heritage of the city's founders.

Just before turning off of Milwaukee Street onto Wisconsin Street there is a trailhead parking lot with restrooms. There is a historic marker in front of the County Courthouse you pass on Wisconsin Street documenting a riot that occurred at that site in resistance to the military draft initiated for the Civil War. It is an interesting read worth stopping for. Also on this street you pass the restored turn of the century Port Hotel. And, conveniently located next to the hotel is the Vines to Cellars Winery.

Exiting downtown Port Washington, as you turn off Jackson

Street back onto the OIT, you experience something you haven't ridden in a while, an incline. It isn't anything to stress out over but compared to the flat terrain the LMT has followed thus far it is fair to rate it as a climb.

It is a little puzzling when the OIT ends at the Hales Trail crossing (which is a road and not a trail). You will need to continue straight on Kaiser Drive for a short stretch before the trail picks up once again. If you were riding through and weren't aware of this ahead of time it might be confusing, at least it was for me.

Use caution at the crossing for Seven Hills Road, it's a pretty busy highway. Once across the road the bike path parallels the highway for a while before you are routed back onto the shoulder of the highway. You will also pass the Country Inn Suites on this stretch.

Once you have circled around under Interstate 43, you return once again to another long uninterrupted stretch the OIT. I wish more civic leaders supported separated bike paths and realized how they contribute to the overall health of a community. I meet people all the time riding on these paths who would not even consider bicycling on highways. So if a separated bike path is what it takes to get people to exercise, then I think it is a worthwhile investment for improving the fitness of our country. If you agree be sure to tell you congressman.

WARNING: On your approach for the town of Belgium, at the first siting of the buildings, stop and walk your bicycle. There is a very rough railroad crossing just prior to entering town that might put a fully loaded touring bike out of commission. Seriously, unless it has been fixed it by the time you ride through it could cause some damage.

Conveniently located near the crossing in Belgium you will find a hardware store that sells sodas/snacks and a bar & grill that serves food. If you are looking for something more substantial in the way of food or a place to stay, head east on Main Street for about a mile. This is also the direction you ride to reach the Luxemburg American Cultural Society Center, where you can learn about the area's roots to the country of Luxemburg.

Once you exit Belgium the OIT routes you along fields of some large scale farming operations. Farming rules in this area. This is evident when you see more caution signs for tractors crossing the trail at intersections than you do automobiles.

If you would like a quick tour of Cedar Grove, and also locate a place to eat, exit left off of the OIT on Main Street. Within the next half a mile ride you will pass a couple of eating establishments, and then you can turn right on Union Avenue to rejoin the OIT.

Oostburg is one of the many Wisconsin towns that have painted warnings across an entire lane of the highway stating "bikes may take entire lane". Wow, Wisconsin really takes care of their bicyclists.

When County Road V turns left to overlap with 12th Street, continue straight on Beach Park Lane if you would like to visit the Kohler-Andrea State Park. The park has camping, beaches, a nature center, and hiking trails.

After passing the turn for the park, as you ride along tree lined 12th Street, you pass the Sheboygan Indian Mound Park. This is an interesting stop; a walking trail among various effigy mounds with informational markers and also an open mound display that demonstrates the flexed type of burial practiced by that culture. To reach the entrance to the park, turn right on Panther Avenue, then right on 9th Street.

While riding along Lake Shore Drive it's nice once again to have views of Lake Michigan. Stop at General King Park to enjoy a snack on the beach as you admire the Great Lake's blue waters and the lighthouse guarding the entrance to Sheboygan River, which you will soon be riding across.

Camping

*Kohler-Andrae State Park
1020 Beach Park Ln
Sheboygan, WI
920-451-4080

Lodging

Courtyard Milwaukee North
5200 W Brown Deer Rd
Brown Deer, WI
414-355-7500

Mequon Country Inn
10240 Cedarburg/Hwy 57
Mequon, WI
262-242-8000

Stagecoach Inn B&B
W61 N520 Washington Ave
Cedarburg, WI
262-375-0208

Baymont Inn & Suites
1415 Port Washington Rd
Grafton, WI
262-387-1180

Port Hotel Inn
101 E Main St
Port Washington, WI
262-377-6195

Holiday Inn
135 E Grand Ave
Port Washington, WI
262-284-9461

*Country Inn Suites
350 E Seven Hills Rd
Port Washington, WI
262-284-2100

Regency Inn
120 Lakeview Dr
Belgium, WI
262-285-3566

Lakeview Motel
N666 Cty Rd LI
Cedar Grove, WI
920-668-6231

*Sleep Inn Suites
3912 Motel Rd
Sheboygan, WI
920-694-0099

Americinn
3664 S Taylor Dr
Sheboygan, WI
920-208-8130

Blue Harbor Resort
725 Blue Harbor Dr
Sheboygan, WI
920-208-3462

Bike Shops

Extreme Ski & Bike
235 N. Main St
Thienville, WI
262-242-1442
(close to OIT)

Zuzu Pedals
228 N Franklin St
Port Washington, WI
262-988-4099
(close to LMT)

Wolf's Cycling
1702 S 12th St
Sheboygan, WI
920-457-0664

Glendale to Sheboygan (53 miles)

Miles N/S	Directions	Dist	R	Service	Miles S/N
0	S to cross Green Tree Rd to cont on OLT (*Glendale)	0.5	P		53
1	L at SS on Good Hope Rd	0.3	5		52
1	R on N Green Bay Ave/SH57	1.0	4		52
2	L into Brown Deer Park then R at SS after entering park	0.6	2		51
2	R on Brown Deer Tr (BDT)	0.2	P		50
3	VR at intersestion cont BDT/OLT	1.1	P		50
4	L then VR after crossing Brown Deer Rd to cont on BDT/OLT	1.1	P		49
5	S at SS to cross W County Line Rd to begin Ozaukee Interurban Tr (OIT)	3.0	P		48
8	*Mequon (Cont on OIT)	4.4	P	GQR	45
12	*Cedarburg (Cont on OIT)	1.5	P	GQR	40
14	L on 1st Ave (*Grafton)	0.7	2		39
14	R on Spring St	0.5	3		38
15	L on 9th Ave	0.1	3		38
15	R at SS on North St	0.1	3		38
15	L on OIT	1.8	P		38
17	R at SS on Terminal Rd	0.2	3		36
17	L on OIT	3.4	P		36
21	Cross Spring St then L to parallel it	0.3	P		32
21	R on Oakland Ave	0.2	3		32
21	L on Park St	0.2	3		32
21	R on OIT	0.4	P		31
22	VL on Milwaukee St (*Port Washington)	0.1	3		31
22	L on Wisconsin St	0.3	3		31
22	R on Pier St	0.2	3	R	31
22	L on Harbor View Ln then R on Jackson St	0.2	3		30
22	L on OIT	0.9	P		30
23	S at SS on Kaiser Dr	0.0	3		29
23	S on OIT	0.6	P		29
24	S at SS to cross Seven Hills Rd/CR LL then R on OIT	0.3	P		29
24	S on CR LL when OIT ends	0.3	3		28
25	L on to ride under overpass then L on Highland Dr	0.4	3		28
25	L on OIT to circle and pass under Highland Dr	6.0	P		28

31	VR R on Main St then L to continue on OIT (*Belgium)	5.0	P	LQR	22
36	R on Cedar Ave then L on Commerce St (*Cedar Grove)	0.4	2	LR	17
36	S to cross Union Ave to cont OIT	3.0	P		16
39	R on De Master Rd	0.1	3		13
39	L at SS on Dewitt Rd/10th St (*Oostburg)	0.4	2	GQR	13
40	L at SS on Center Ave then R to cont on 10th St/CR A	3.5	2	R	13
43	R at SS on CR V	2.1	3		9
45	R to cont on CR V	1.9	3	R	7
47	L to cont on CR V/12th St	3.6	2	CQ	5
51	R on Humboldt Ave	0.5	2		2
51	L at SS on Lake Shore Dr/7th St	1.1	2		1
53	L at SS on Indiana Ave	0.1	3		0
53	R on 8th St (*Sheboygan)		3		0

There are some large farming operations in this area.

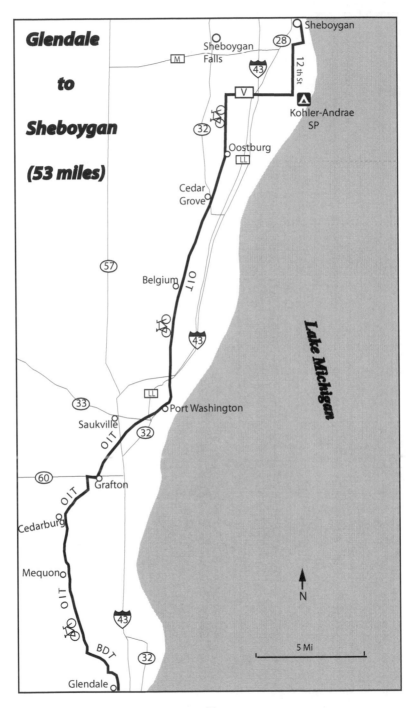

Glendale

to

Sheboygan

(53 miles)

Sheboygan

Sheboygan Falls

M

28

43

V

12th St

Kohler-Andrae SP

32

Oostburg

LL

Cedar Grove

57

Belgium

OIT

43

LL

Port Washington

33

Saukville

32

OIT

60

OIT

Grafton

Cedarburg

Mequon

OIT

43

BDT

32

Glendale

Lake Michigan

N

5 Mi

Lake Michigan Trail
SECTION 6

Sheboygan to Two Creeks (49 miles)

This section begins with the 8th Street Bridge routing you over scenic Sheboygan River. You then follow Riverfront Road along the pier, past several restaurants and the Sheboygan Bicycle Company. Sheboygan is another enjoyable city to tour on a bicycle, with its historic buildings lining the streets of the downtown district and the waterfront area; however, this city has something that you won't find in the other cities we've visited: what Travel & Leisure magazine refers to as one of the "World's Greatest Public Bathrooms!" The John Michael Kohler Arts Center has taken art to a new level, or to be more accurate, a new locale: the washroom.

The Arts Center commissioned local artists to turn their six public washrooms into independent works of art. Truly, words cannot do justice to the end results of their creative efforts. You have to visit the Arts Center to appreciate it. It's only a short ride off the LMT and it is worth the ride. To reach the center, at the turn for Pennsylvania Avenue continue straight on North 6th Street for another two blocks. You then turn left on New York Avenue. The entrance is half a block away. Admission is by voluntary donation, and don't worry about stopping to only visit the washrooms, believe me, you won't be the first visitors to do that.

Another unique experience, if you don't mind riding all the way across Sheboygan, is the Kohler factory tour and museum. The tour includes visits to the production line, the design area, and museum, which tells the history of the nation's largest plumbing-ware manufacturer. It is an interesting place to spend some time. Reservations are required by phoning 920-457-3699.

You exit Sheboygan on a separated bike path that runs alongside the lakeshore. The path parallels Broughton Drive, pass Deland Park and the North Side Municipal Beach. These are both welcome sites to stop for a swim to cool off or just a respite from your ride.

The restaurants in Cleveland are about a mile off the LMT, to the left on Washington Avenue. The lodging listed in the guidebook is located at a ramp off Interstate 43, about a mile further on the other side of town.

Lakeshore Road passes Whistling Straight Golf Club along this stretch. I no longer chase a little white ball around a well-manicured landscape, but for those who do you will probably want to check out this picturesque PGA Championship course.

This is a nice long ride on Lakeshore Road. Once you exit the suburbs you are back in farm country. When I rode through I saw huge flocks of birds out in the fields. There will be an even better opportunity for viewing wildlife later on this stretch when you reach Fischer Creek Conservation Area. The dense trees of the conservation area butt right up against the shoulder of the highway.

On your approach to Manitowoc you pass a unique disc golf course, located at Silver Creek Park. It is a very challenging course with holes located along creek banks, on hillsides, beside natural dune sand traps, and at the edge of an 80-foot drop off.

If, like most people, you don't have time for an extended bike tour around all of Lake Michigan, consider splitting your tour into two separate trips. By utilizing the SS Badger Ferry to shuttle across the center of the lake you could tour the lower half of the LMT on one trip, and then return at another date to use the ferry for a tour of the upper half. The great part about this is that it wouldn't require a vehicle shuttle, because you will be leaving your vehicle at the start/finish for both tours. It's great when things just seem to work out. To reach the ferry entrance, turn right off 8th Street onto Madison Street.

After crossing the Manitowoc River, take an immediate right onto the Mariner Trail (MT). The Maritime Museum is located next to the trailhead parking lot. The Best Western Lakefront Hotel is located near the start also.

The MT routes cyclists right along the shoreline, on what the locals claim is "the longest uninterrupted view of Lake Michigan in the state of Wisconsin." It is a sweet ride. You pass several historic markers, an optional side trip to a lighthouse, and also one of my favorite tour stops, a Dairy Queen. However, if you're unable to eat ice cream twice in the same day you might want to wait a few more miles to save yourself for a really special treat.

Two Rivers is a unique town with two rivers running through the downtown district. What's even more interesting, at least to me, is that the rivers are named Twin Rivers, however, each one has a different place of origin and are different in length. So where did the name Twin Rivers come from? This would be good material for an Abbott and Costello skit. To the citizens of Two Rivers, I'm just kidding. I enjoyed my visit in your beautiful town.

For those of you who had the willpower to bypass a stop at the Dairy Queen, or, like me, you believe there is always room for ice cream, stop at the Washington House Museum at 1622 Jefferson Street. Once there, belly up to the bar at the replica of the 1880s Ed Berners' Ice Cream Parlor to enjoy Mr. Berners' original invention, "the ice cream sundae." While enjoying your treat, read their brochure about the interesting story behind the inspiration for this desert sensation, and also where it's miss-spelling originated. I won't say any more about it because I don't want to spoil it for you.

The Washington House was built in the 1850s and was originally a hotel. It has a very stylish interior, with the original decorative tin ceiling and beautiful mural-walled ballroom. So be sure to allow time for a visit to the ice cream parlor, the building, and the museum.

After leaving downtown Two Rivers on Zlatnik Drive, take advantage of the concrete bike path on the right that borders the public beach. The bike path makes for a nice ride but be sure to watch for the left turn into Neshotah Park. After crossing the park's parking lot you begin riding the Rawley's Point Recreation Trail (RPRT). The trail is hard packed crushed stone, however if you prefer avoiding this surface, shortly after beginning the trail you will have the option to ride on highways which the trail parallels.

When you reach the Sandy Ridge Drive crossing, immediately after turning left you will see where the trail resumes across the street on the right. Shortly after this you cross Sandy Bay Road, where you will discover that the condition of the RPRT dramatically deteriorates. It isn't much more than a hiking trail at this point. If there has been any recent precipitation you are going to be taking your bike for a hike through here. You have the option of avoiding this section of the trail by riding Sandy Bay Road. The highway parallels the trail all the way to the entrance for the Point Beach State Forest on Park Road.

I want to note that the stretch of RPRT after crossing Sandy Bay Road is the worst section of the trail. So if that doesn't discourage you, then go for it. If you do remain on the trail there are some good opportunities for stealth camping, although I am not advocating this. I just know that some cyclists enjoy this, so I'm just pointing it out.

When the RPRT reaches Park Road, turn left to continue the LMT, or turn right to enter Point Beach State Park. The park has camping, primitive cabins, concessions, a beach, and the Rawley Point Lighthouse.

On this next section of the Lakeshore Road you ride pass massive corn fields. If it is windy, the tall stalks make for a good wind break. As you are pedaling along Nuclear Road, checkout the cute silhouette cutouts on the side of the barn of a woman chasing a cowboy with a rolling pin. Lol!

FYI, Two Creeks has no services.

Camping

Seagull Marina CG
1400 Lake St
Two Rivers, WI
920-793-3321

Scheffel's Hideway CG
6511 Cty Rd O
Two Rivers, WI
920-657-1270

Point Beach State Forest
9400 Cty Rd O
Two Rivers, WI
920-794-7480

Lodging

Harbor Winds Motel
908 S 8th St
Sheboygan, WI
920-452-9000

Econo Lodge
723 Central Ave
Sheboygan, WI
920-458-1400

*Lake Orchard Farms B&B
N9214 Cty Rd Ls
Sheboygan, WI
920-693-8348
(12 miles north of town)

Econo Lodge
908 Washington St
Manitowoc, WI
920-682-8271
(1 blk off LMT)

*Best Western Lakefront Hotel
101 Maritime Dr
Manitowoc, WI
920-430-9014

Westport B&B
635 N 8th St
Manitowoc, WI
920-686-0465

*Village Inn on the Lake
3310 Memorial Dr
Two Rivers, WI
920-794-8818

*Lakeview Motel
2792 Memorial Dt
Two Rivers, WI
920-793-2251

*Lighthouse Inn
1515 Memorial Dr
Two Rivers, WI
920-793-4524

Bike Shops

Sheboygan Bicycle Company
721 River Dr
Sheboygan, WI
920-208-8735

Johnnie;s Bike Shop
1001 Michigan Ave
Sheboygan, WI
920-452-0934

The Fitness Store
1410 Dewey St
Manitowoc, WI
920-684-8088

*Broken Spoke Bicycle Studio
1010 Washington St
Manitowoc, WI
920-652-0950

*Heavy Pedals Blcycles
826 S 8th St
Manitowoc. WI
920-652-0888

*Broken Spoke Bicycle Studio
1200 Washington St
Two Rivers, WI
920-553-1950

Sheboygan to Two Creeks (49 miles)

Miles N/S	Directions	Dist	R	Service	Miles S/N
0	R at SL 8th St (*Sheboygan)	0.4	3		49
0	R at SL on Riverfront Rd	0.4	3	R	48
1	R at SS on Pennsylvania Ave	0.2	3		48
1	L on Broughton Dr	1.4	P		48
2	R on Barrett St/Park Ave	0.3	P		46
3	R at SS on 3rd St/North Ave	0.9	3		46
4	R at SS on 8th St	0.6	3		45
4	L on Eisner Ave	0.6	3		45
5	R on Lakeshore Rd	8.8	3		44
14	R on Cleveland Rd (*Cleveland)	0.2	3	GLR	35
14	L on Lakeshore Dr	9.0	3		35
23	S on 10th St	3.7	3	QR	26
27	R on Columbus St (*Manitowoc)	0.1	3	GLQR	22
27	L at SS on 8th St	0.7	3		22
27	R after crossing Manitowoc River to begin Mariner Tr	5.9	P	LQR	21
33	S on Washington St	0.1	3	CR	16
	*Two Rivers			GLQR	15
33	R on River St	0.1	3		15
33	L on Jefferson St	0.1	3	R	15
34	R at SS 17th St	0.4	2		15
34	L on Zlatnik Dr then R on pave bike trail	0.3	3		15
34	L to enter Neshotah Park and begin Rawley's Point Rec Tr (RPRT)	0.1	P		15
34	R to parallel Pierce St on RPRT	0.1	P		14
34	S to cross 22nd St then R on RPRT	0.5	P		14
35	Cross Sandy Ridge Dr then L and R to cont RPRT	0.8	P		14
36	S to cross Sandy Bay Rd/CR O	3.9	P	C	13
40	L on Park Rd	0.1	1	CRL	9
41	R at SS CR O	1.7	3		9
41	L on CR V	0.9	3		7
42	R on Lakeshore Rd	2.2	3		6
44	L on Nuclear Rd	1.4	3		4
46	R at SS on SH 42	2.8	3		3
49	VL on Nero Rd (*Two Creeks)		2		0

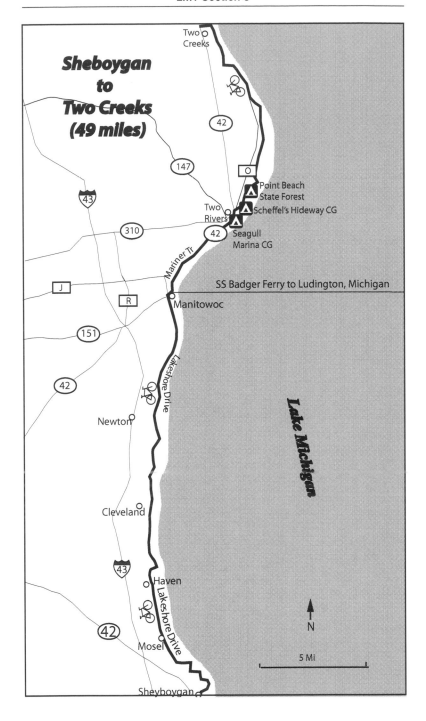

Sheboygan
to
Two Creeks
(49 miles)

Two Creeks

42

147

43

310

Two Rivers

42

Mariner Tr

Point Beach State Forest

Scheffel's Hideway CG

Seagull Marina CG

J

R

Manitowoc

SS Badger Ferry to Ludington, Michigan

151

42

Newton

Lakeshore Drive

Lake Michigan

Cleveland

43

Haven

Lakeshore Drive

42

Mosel

Sheyboygan

N

5 Mi

Lake Michigan Trail
SECTION 7

Two Creeks to Sturgeon Bay (53 miles)

If you are in a hurry, and would prefer riding a more direct route for this section than the one described in the Mileage Log within this guidebook, rather than veering left on Nero Road, remain on State Highway 42. You can follow it all the way to Sturgeon Bay. The description in the Mileage Log routes cyclists along quiet country roads, past tranquil farmland, and along the scenic lakeshore. So if this doesn't appeal to you, you have an option.

When you reach the right turn onto Sandy Bay Road, if you are enjoying your ride through this rural setting and would like an opportunity to expand the experience, consider a stay at the historic Norman General Store B&B. With just a two mile ride after turning left on Sandy Bay Road and then another mile to your right on Norman Road, hosts Ann and Jerry Sinkula will enrich your visit with tales of the history for the area, which dates back to the 1850s when Bohemian immigrants first began to settle here. The couple are lifelong local residents, first as dairy farmers and now as inn hosts. They welcome the occasion to assist you in planning your activities to explore the rich ethnic heritage of the area.

As I was riding along Lakeview Road, I sensed that life in one of the homes along the highway would be a lot like living on the seacoast. The homes are perched high on a bluff offering expansive views across the lake. And just as the oceans do, the body of water is so large that the curvature of the earth blocks the view of the opposite shore. Until this tour I did not realize how large Lake Michigan actually is.

Kewaunee is another picturesque lake harbor village the LMT routes cyclists through. When the community was founded in the middle 1880s its forefathers had ambitions that their city would rival Chicago as Lake Michigan's premier port. At its peak in 1892, the first auto ferry across Lake Michigan was established here.

As a result of this early prosperity, wealthy timber growers and business owners desired large homes farther from the congestion of the downtown area. This resulted in a rich collection of architecture displayed in the beautiful homes of the Marquette

51

Historic District. These fine homes have been well maintained over the years with limited alterations to the original structures. Stop by the Kewaunee Chamber of Commerce building, which you pass at 308 North Main Street, to pick up a pamphlet for the Historical District Walking Tour to view these elegant structures. The walking tour makes for a nice riding tour also.

Another must-see on your tour is the Kewaunee Pierhead Lighthouse. Located at the end of a 300 foot pier with an adjacent two story building, the lighthouse is unique from others seen on the LMT.

One final stop, as you depart Kewaunee on Lakeshore drive, is Father Marquette Memorial Park. The park marks the location where the Father offered Holy Sacrifice of Mass on November 1, 1674. He was a member of the expedition led by French-Canadian explorer, Louis Jolliet, to explore a possible trade route down the Mississippi River. I encountered memorials about their adventure while researching the Bicycling Guide to the Mississippi River Trail. Jolliet and Father Marquette travelled all the way down the Mississippi River to the Arkansas River inlet. At that point they encountered evidence that natives had been trading with Europeans. Jolliet turned back for fear of encounters with explorers from Spain.

The park also has restrooms and benches, where you can stop and prepare for the next leg of the trip.

If your destination for the day is the At the Waters Edge B&B listed in the guidebook, when the LMT turns left off of County Road K onto State Highway 42, turn right to ride about half a mile. And yes, it is located at the edge of Lake Michigan. For those wishing to camp, the LMT passes the entrance for Big Lake Campground a little over a tenth of a mile after you begin riding State Highway 42. You will also find a grocery, restaurants, and lodging conveniently located on this stretch of highway. The inviting white sands of Algoma Beach are also conveniently located along Lake Street. What more could a touring cyclist ask for?

On your approach to Sturgeon Bay, Tacoma Beach Road just becomes Oxford Avenue somewhere along the way. After this transition you will reach an intersection with Walnut Street and Shiloh Road. Rather than continuing straight, Oxford Road turns to the right, to cross State Highway 42. You will want to remain on Oxford Road. If you weren't prepared for this it would be tempting to continue straight.

Madison Avenue passes the Door County Maritime on the approach to the bridge over Sturgeon Bay. One of the highlights of the museum is the immaculately restored John Purves tugboat.

They offer tours of the 1919 vintage vessel that has not only provided service in the Great Lakes but also other large bodies of water ranging from the Caribbean to the Bering Sea.

Be sure to use the bike/ped lane on the east side of the Madison Bridge so you can pause to enjoy the view of the activities on Sturgeon Bay. Once across the bay, the LMT once again offers cyclists the opportunity to experience a unique one-of-a-kind adventure. The Holiday Music Motel is the world's only fully operational motel featuring live-music events, collaborative songwriting retreats and a radio station that exclusively broadcasts the music created within their own walls. Even if you are not interested in their commitment in the support of independent artists, the motel is centrally located for an ideal home base for exploring the Sturgeon Bay area. Pickup your "Tour Our Neighborhood" map at the front desk to begin your Sturgeon Bay adventure.

If you would like an sample of what their music is about, you can listen to Steel Bridge Radio, their 24/7 internet radio broadcast, at steelbridgeradio.com. If you enjoy your stay at the motel you will have an opportunity to visit it later in the tour. For after the LMT loops around the Door Peninsula it passes back through Sturgeon Bay on your journey south, around Green Bay. Both routes overlap on the Madison Bridge.

As you ride along Canal Road leaving Sturgeon Bay, pull off at one of the turnouts to view the busy boat traffic in the Sturgeon Bay Shipping Canal. The section of the canal you pass while riding through here is a manmade canal, built in 1881. Private investors constructed the waterway to link Lake Michigan to Sturgeon Bay and on to Green Bay. The 1.3 mile cut cost only $291,000. You couldn't even pay someone to survey it for that price today. The U.S. Army Corps of Engineers maintains it now.

Continue straight on Canal Road when the LMT turns left on Lake Forest Park Road to reach the U.S. Coast Guard and the Sturgeon Bay Canal Lighthouse.

This section states that it ends in Sturgeon Bay; however, it actually terminates about fifteen miles north of town. There were no significant landmarks at the end so I used Sturgeon Bay as a reference point.

Camping

*Kewaunee Marina CG
123 N Main St
Kewaunee, WI
920-388-3300

Kewaunee Village CG & Cabin
333 Terraqua Dr
Kewaunee, WI
920-388-4851

*Big Lake CG
2427 Lake St
Algoma, WI
920-487-2726

Lodging

Norman General Store B&B
E3296 Cty Rd G
Kewaunee, WI
920-388-4580

Coho Motel
795 Main St
Kewaunee, WI
920-388-3565

*Harbor Light Lodge
211 Milwaukee St
Kewaunee, WI
920-388-3700

At the Waters Edge B&B
N7136 SH 42
Algoma, WI
920-203-9584

*Algoma Beach Motel
1500 Lake St
Algoma, WI
920-487-2828

*Harbor Inn Motel
99 Michigan St
Algoma, WI
920-487-5241

*White Birch Inn
1009 S Oxford Ave
Sturgeon Bay, WI
920-743-3295

*Holiday Music Motel
30 N 1st Ave
Sturgeon Bat, WI
920-743-5571

*Snug Harbor Inn
1627 Memorial Dr
Sturgeon Bay, WI
920-743-2337

Bike Shops

Nor Door Sport & Cyclery
60 Madison Ave
Sturgeion Bay, WI
920-818-0803

I never get tired of views like this along the shoreline.

Two Creeks to Sturgeon Bay (53 miles)

Miles N/S	Directions	Dist	R	Service	Miles S/N
0	VL on Nero Rd	1.2	2		53
1	L then R at SS on Woodside Rd	1.9	2		52
3	R on Sandy Bay Rd	1.5	2		50
5	L at SS on Lakeview Rd	6.1	2		48
11	R at SS on SH 42/Milwaukee St	2.2	3	R	42
	*Kewaunee			CGLQR	
13	R on Hathaway Dr	0.3	3		40
13	L on Lakeshore Dr	2.5	3		40
16	R at SS on 1st Rd/Lakeshore Dr	3.3	3		37
19	S at SS on Longfellow Rd	3.2	2		34
22	R at SS on CR K	0.9	3		31
23	L at SS on SH 42/4th St	1.2	2	CGLQR	30
24	VR on Lake St	0.2	3		28
25	R on Clark St	0.1	3		28
25	R on Parkway Ave	0.0	3		28
25	L at SS on Steele St	0.1	3		28
	*Algoma			GLQR	
25	R at SS on 2nd St	0.2	3		28
25	R at SS on Water St/CR S	3.7	3		28
29	R on CR U/Clay Banks Rd	12.3	3		24
41	L on Tacoma Beach Rd/Oxford Ave/Walnut St	0.9	3		12
42	R at SS on Neenah Ave	0.6	3		11
42	L at SS on Maple St	0.1	3		10
43	R at SL on Madison Ave (*Sturgeon Bay)	0.6	3	GLQR	10
43	R at SS on 3rd Ave	0.3	3		10
43	VL on Memorial Dr	1.3	3	L	9
45	L on 18th Pl	0.5	3		8
45	R at SS on Utah St	0.1	3		8
45	R on 20th Pl	0.2	3		7
46	L on Vermont Pl	0.2	3		7
46	R on Cove Rd then L on Canal Rd/CR Tt	2.6	3		7
48	L on CR Tt/Lake Forest Park Rd	3.3	3		4
52	R at SS on CR Tt then L on Lake Michigan Dr	1.1	3		1
53	R at SS on CR T/Glidden Dr		3	L	0

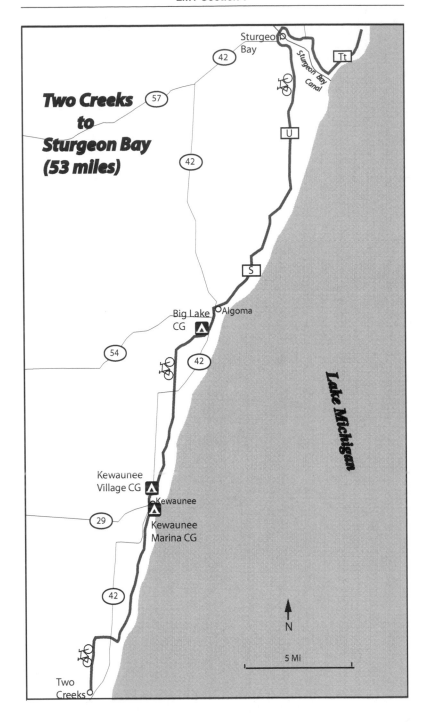

Two Creeks to Sturgeon Bay (53 miles)

Sturgeon Bay

42

57

42

Tt

U

S

Big Lake CG

Algoma

54

42

Kewaunee Village CG

Kewaunee

29

Kewaunee Marina CG

42

Lake Michigan

Sturgeon Bay Canal

N

5 Mi

Two Creeks

Lake Michigan Trail
SECTION 8

Sturgeon Bay to Ellison Bay (41 miles)

The vegetation and forest is so thick and close to the highway through the beginning of this section that it almost feels like you're riding an extra wide bike path. Riding through this wooded area with occasional peeks of Lake Michigan makes for a sweet ride. But don't get too relaxed, the dense trees and winding roads create blind corners for motorists. Use caution.

I couldn't decide if the homes tucked back in the trees on the lakeshore are weekend retreats or fulltime retirement homes. Based on the entertaining names they have given their "little piece of paradise" the residents have the right attitude to enjoy themselves when they are here.

When approaching the end of Glidden Drive you have your choice of a couple of very nice places to stay. I'm talking very nice, with some pretty high rates to go with it. But sometimes you want to treat yourself to a nice place. So I've included one of them in the guidebook.

As Bark Road crosses Whitefish Bay Road the pavement continues straight on Cave Point Drive. The map I had showed that this road continues through to join Clark Lake Road. I followed the Cave Point Drive a couple miles before the pavement stopped and a rough hiking trail picked up. It was hike-a-bike type of terrain. This was not something I was equipped to ride that day, and I recommend that unless you are on a mountain bike, with no load, that you turn around also. I met a group of friendly ladies who were walking the trail and they said this was the boundary for Whitefish Dunes State Park.

Your eating options have been slim for a while, so you might be ready for a stop at the Hitching Post Bar & Grill, located on Whitefish Bay Road, to load up on some calories.

I don't mean to be plugging these B&Bs, (I am not rewarded for including them in the guidebook) but the LMT passes another nice one I have listed in the guidebook that is a pretty unique place to stay. The 1908 Whitefish Bay Farm is a working sheep farm, an art gallery, and a B&B. Your stay includes a made-from-scratch breakfast with ingredients grown on site, a tour of the farm, followed by a visit to the art gallery located in the granary barn. You can then relax in the morning, sipping a hot beverage, while watching sheep grazing on the hillside. What a relaxing experience.

The Whitefish Dunes State Park entrance is conveniently located at the intersection of Clarks Lake Road and Schauer Road. Regretfully, it does not have camping, but it is a great place to take a break from the road. There are clean sandy beaches, a nature center, a self-guided hiking trail, plus informative guided hikes through wetlands and sandy beach dunes lead by their resident naturalist. There are also three reconstructed village sites located at the center. Each village exemplifies living conditions for the visitors who have resided in the area during different periods dating all the way back to AD 100.

Shortly after passing the entrance to the state park you pass the Cave Point County Park. This is a roadside park with restrooms, picnic tables, and a historical kiosk. Perched high on a bluff, it offers excellent views across Lake Michigan. You are also able to see large sea caves in the limestone cliffs, created by the constant pounding of the surf. I wish there was a campground here because I would enjoy listening to the waves crashing across the bluff while snuggled in my sleeping bag.

A table with a view for lunch break at Cave Point County Park.

Keep an eye out on your left as you ride Schauer Road. There is a house that has a wide assortment of art works on display in the front lawn. This is one of the pleasant spontaneous discoveries you find during a tour that I like to refer to as "Travelers' eye candy".

There was no sign for the turn for Lake Shore Road when I rode through. Use the distance in the log Mileage Log to locate the turn.

You have a wide choice of motels in Bailey's Harbor. Plus there are a variety of attractions to entertain you if you are looking for a place to layover for a day or two. There is camping, a beach, and plenty of good eating places. It is only a short ride to the Ridges Sanctuary, where you can visit the nature center, a pair of lighthouses, and the highlight of a visit, a naturalist-led hike through the preserve to learn about the unique flora and interesting history of the refuge and its founders.

For something different, try a kayak tour on Bailey's Harbor, where in the shallow clear water you will be able to view wrecked schooners dating back to the 1800s. Visit the Tourist Information Center at 2392 Country Road F to collect information for planning your adventure.

After leaving Bailey's Harbor, it's just a short side trip to visit one of the more interesting lighthouses on the trip. The Cana Island Lighthouse is actually located on an island. You have to walk across a beach causeway to reach it. As you tour the isolated grounds of the 8.7 acre island, it's easy to imagine what life was like when the lighthouse keeper and his family lived there. As you hike the 97 steps of the spiral staircase within the lighthouse tower, think of what it was like over 140 years ago, when nightly the keeper climbed these same steps carrying heated lard to keep the light burning. Once you reach the gallery deck at the top of the 89-foot tower be sure to take time to enjoy the 360-degree view. There is a charge to visit the lighthouse, however all the money from admission and the gift store goes toward maintaining the facilities.

As you are riding on Scandia Road, if you are in need of supplies, instead of turning right on Birchwood Drive you may continue straight for about half a mile to reach Sisters Bay. If you are not in need of supplies, just continue on the LMT. You will have an opportunity to visit the village on the return route.

The small towns located in the bays and harbors on the Door Peninsula are the very definition of the phrase, "quaint and picturesque communities". These special places have successfully preserved the timeless ambiance that has made the area a popular retreat for over a hundred years. Part of the reason for this is the personal touch that comes from having most of the restaurants and lodging locally owned and operated. It seems the chain franchises have not ventured onto the peninsula, and I found this a welcome respite.

Ellison Bay is a good example of what I am talking about. You can get a nice clean room for a reasonable rate, and the owner will probably be the person who checks you in. Then, after a short pleasant walk you can grab a fine meal at the Viking Grill, and possibly be served by the owners or a member of their family. Following this, you might decide to visit the hard cider tasting room at the Island Orchard Cider House. As you sip samples of their latest creations, the owners will be more than happy to share the story of how they developed their passion for brewing cider while on family visits to Brittany, France. As they became more interested in the process this led them on trips to Normandy, where cider was first created during the Middle Ages.

Areas like Ellison Bay and others the LMT passes along the tour of Door Peninsula have a way of encouraging visitors to slow down to enjoy the simpler pleasures in life.

The LMT passes back through Ellison Bay as it backtracks from the northern point of the peninsula. I tried to list different lodging opportunities on the return ride, so you might check the next section for more services to choose from.

To reach the entrance for Wagon Trail Campground, turn right off Mike River Road onto Country Road Zz and ride about half a mile. Continue past the turn for the campground another half a mile to arrive at Rowley's Bay Resort.

Camping

Bailey's Grove CG
2552 County Rd F
Baileys Harbor, WI
920-839-2559

Beantown CG
8398 County Rd F
Baileys Harbor. WI
920-839-1439

Aqualand Camp Resort
2445 County Rd Q
Sister Bay, WI
920-854-4573

Wagon Trail CG
1190 County Rd Zz
Ellison Bay, WI
920-854-4818

Lodging

*Glidden Lodge Resort
4676 Glidden Dr
Sturgeon Bay, WI
920-748-3900

*Whitefish Bay Farm B&B
3831 Clark Laek Rd
Sturgeon Bay, WI
920-743-1560

*Inlet Motel
6269 SH 57
Jacksonport, WI
920-823-2499

*Square Rigger Lodge
6332 SH 57
Jacksonport, WI
920-823-2404

*Square Rigger Harbor Motel
7950 SH 57
Baileys Harbor, WI
920-839-2016

*Beach Front Motel
8040 SH 57
Baileys Harbor, WI
920-839-2345

*Cedar Tree Cottages
1825 Waters End Rd
Sister Bay, WI
920-854-4865

Rowleys Bay Resort
1041 County Rd Zz
Ellison Bay, WI
920-854-2385

Bayview Resort
12030 Cedar Rd
Ellison Bay, WI
920-854-2006

Bike Shops

N/A

Sturgeon Bay to Ellison Bay (41 Miles)

Miles N/S	Directions	Dist	R	Service	Miles S/N
0	R at SS on CR T/Glidden Dr	5.8	3	L	41
6	R on Bark Rd	0.6	2		35
6	L on Whitefish Bay Rd/ CR T	0.5	3	R	34
7	R on Nelson Ln	1.1	2		34
8	R at SS on Clarks Lake Rd	2.4	3	L	33
10	S on Schauer Rd	2.2	3		30
13	R at SS on Cave Point Dr	1.1	3		28
14	R on Jorns Rd	0.1	3		27
14	L on Lake Shore Rd (unsigned)	0.8	3		27
	*Jacksonport			GLR	26
15	R at SS on SH 57	7.0	3	R	26
	*Bailey's Harbor			CGLQR	19
22	S on SH 57	1.0	3	LQR	19
23	R on CR Q	8.1	3		18
31	R on Woodcrest Rd	2.4	3	C	10
33	L at SS on Scandia Rd	0.2	3		8
	*Sister Bay			GLQR	7
33	R on Birchwood Dr	0.2	2		7
33	R on Trillium Ln	0.3	2		7
34	L at SS on Hill Rd then R on Hillcrest Rd	0.5	2		7
34	R at SS on Waters End Rd	3.0	3		6
37	L on Mink River Rd	3.4	3	C	3
41	S at SS to cross SH 42 on Cedar Shore Rd		3	QR	0
	*Ellison Bay			GLQR	

61

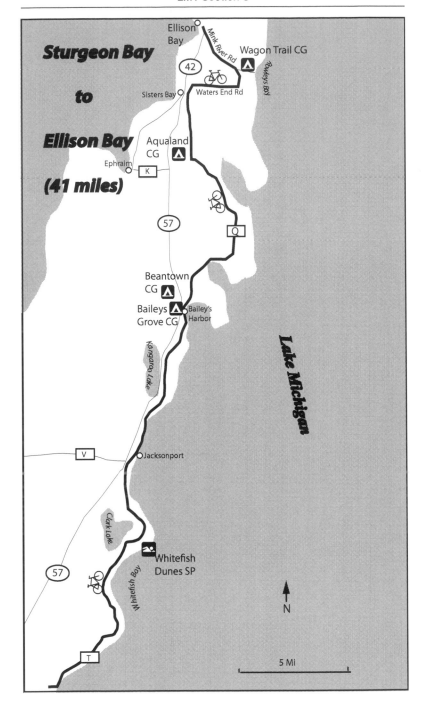

Sturgeon Bay

to

Ellison Bay

(41 miles)

Ellison Bay

Wagon Trail CG

Mink River Rd

Rowleys Bay

42

Sisters Bay

Waters End Rd

Aqualand CG

Ephraim

K

57

Q

Beantown CG

Baileys Grove CG

Bailey's Harbor

Kangaroo Lake

Lake Michigan

V

Jacksonport

Clark Lake

57

Whitefish Dunes SP

Whitefish Bay

N

5 Mi

T

Lake Michigan Trail
SECTION 9

Ellison Bay to Sturgeon Bay (70 miles)

Looking at the map for this section you realize just how remote your ride to the extreme northern apex of the Door Peninsula is going to be. Bordered on three sides by the waters of Lake Michigan and Green Bay, this narrow strip of land is pretty isolated from the rest of the continent. I'm sure this isolation contributed to the preservation of the charm and character of the communities you travel through along the LMT route.

At the intersection for Garrett Bay Road, a one block detour to your right will take you to the Island Orchard Cider House where you can pick up a bottle of hard cider for the road. Cider, cheese, crackers, and sardines, sitting on a beach watching the waves roll in, that's the kind of lunch that most people only dream about experiencing. If you delay your lunch until you reach the boat landing on Garrett Bay Road, you can also view the skeleton of the schooner, *Fleetwing* that sank here in 1888.

Also located along this road is The Clearing Folk School, "your place to slow down, renew, and reconnect." Founded in 1935, it was created as a place where ordinary people could go to "clear one's mind." Stop to see if your visit coincides with one of the classes or education programs that regularly take place at the site. Also, check their schedule for future events, keeping in mind that you will be passing through here on your return ride.

In case you didn't notice it on the map, the LMT north of Ellison Bay is an out-and-back ride. So if you miss something on your ride north, you will have a second chance to catch it on your ride back south.

Traffic is low on these highways. The only vehicles you'll encounter here are for people with the northern end of the Door Peninsula as their destination, because no one is passing through here on their way to somewhere else. I don't know if it's psychological or what, but I felt more isolated from the mainland while riding the northern part of the peninsula, but this feeling only contributed to the adventure.

There are a number of choices for lodging along this stretch, several which I have listed in the guidebook. There are also area attractions you may want to visit, such as the Door County Maritime Museum, just outside of Gills Rock. Another traditional stop for visitors to the area is Bea's Ho-Made Products. The Landins family has been making their award winning jams, jellies, pickles, and other specialties at this homestead for four generations. You should be able to find several delicious treats to compliment your hard cider at lunch.

During your ride along State Highway 42, outside of Gills Rock, you might notice a sign for Newport State Park. It is about a four mile ride to the park entrance, and the camping is hike-in sites only.

When State Highway 42 literally runs into Lake Michigan, for those wanting to take their escape from the mainland to another level, you can hitch-a-ride on the half-hour ferry ride to Washington Island. This isn't actually considered part of the LMT, but I've included an optional guide in the following segment to assist those seeking a Washington Island Adventure.

Once you have dipped your front wheel in the waters at Northport, steer your trusty steed about and begin your return trip. I have reversed the directions in the Mileage Logs to match the directions for the turns now riding from the north; however, it is the same route back to Ellison Bay. But if you are like me, riding from the opposite direction everything looks different, so it will seem like a new route.

Upon reaching Ellison Bay you exit by a different route than the one you originally entered on your ride north. You will pass a couple more motels outside of town along State Highway 42, and also a county park.

It is a pleasant ride to Sister Bay, with a decent shoulder and moderate traffic. Sister Bay is a resort town wrapped around the shores of a bay. The village has every service a weary cyclist might need, except for a bicycle shop. After a hot day of riding it's hard to beat a stop at the Door County Ice Cream Factory. With over 30 flavors of homemade ice cream and homemade waffle cones, this might be considered a must-stop.

Ephraim has a quaint European village atmosphere to it, with its Swiss chalet style architecture and the tall steeples of the churches. There is also a wide assortment of art galleries in this area. I believe the remoteness of the Door Peninsula must attract artists.

Allow extra time for your ride through the Peninsula State Park. Even if you aren't camping in the park there are plenty of attractions you will want to spend time exploring. Something I really enjoyed was the 250' Eagle Terrace Tower. Built in 1914, the tower was constructed with trees cut within the park, without the aid of machinery. The deck at the top of the tower offers a magnificent sprawling view of the harbor and the islands just off the shoreline. I saw a sailboat on Nicolet Bay, anchored in a sheltered cove at Horseshoe Island. The idea of just dropping anchor anywhere you want and calling it home for the night sounds really appealing to me. Maybe next time I'll tour Lake Michigan via sailboat.

The park also has hiking trails, historical recordings of Native Americans dating as far back as 500 BC, a well preserved lighthouse, and many other fun activities to make your visit an interesting one. Plus, they have camping. I'll ride out of my way and adjust my schedule to camp at state and national parks over commercial ones.

On the ride along Cottage Row check out the rustic long stone walls bordering the highway. These were probably built before the use of heavy machinery, so someone put in a lot of long hours of backbreaking work to build these. This was another area where I couldn't determine if these were weekend retreats or permanent homes.

As you continue your ride along the Green Bay shoreline, through the resort communities of Fish Creek and Egg Harbor, you're nearing the end of your Door Peninsula tour. You will have plenty of opportunities for services through this area, and the traffic isn't so heavy as to distract from your ride. There are also several roadside parks for you to take a needed break. Of particular interest along Bay Shore Drive, was the George K. Pinney County Park Marina. The park is located at the base of the massive rock quarry where most of the rock used to build the homes and stone fences you've been seeing came from. Stop to read the historical marker about the interesting history of the quarry.

Riding through Sturgeon Bay from the north provides a different perspective from that on your ride up from the south, however you will be in familiar territory when you reach the Madison Street Bridge across Sturgeon Bay. Remember to avoid the metal grid on the bridge by using the sidewalk.

Once across the bridge it won't be long before you are back into farm country again. To reach the entrance of the Potawatomi State Park, at the left turn onto Sand Bay Road, continue straight another tenth of a mile on Park Drive. Only a few miles further along Sand Bay Road, The Jelly Stone Park Campground offers another camping opportunity, with a left turn onto May Road. Also, only a few miles past this, the Countryside Motel has camping. It's been awhile since there has been a choice of places to camp along this trail.

You finish this section with an enjoyable ride along the shores of Little Sturgeon Bay. And, once again, the true end of the section does not match the city listed in the heading due to a lack of reference point for the real termination.

Camping

*Hy-Land Park RV Park
11563 Hwy 42
Ellison Bay, WI
920-854-4850

Egg Harbor CG & RV
8164 Hwy 42
Egg Harbor, WI
920-868-3278

Monument Point CG
5718 Monument Point Rd
Sturgeon Bay, WI
920-743-9411
(1 mile off Bay Shore Dr)

*Potawatomi SP
County Road PD
Sturgeon Bay, WI
920-746-2890

*Jellystone Park CG
3677 May Rd
Sturgeon Bay, WI
920-743-9001
(Just off Sand Bay Rd)

*Countryside Motel & CG
3120 Stevenson Pier Rd
Sturgeon Bay, WI
920-824-5309

Lodging

*Parkside Inn
11946 Hwy 42
Ellison Bat, WI
920-854-5221

*Hillside Inn
11934 Hwy 42
Ellison Bay, WI
920-854-2928

*Shoreline Resort
12747 Hwy 42
Gills Rock, WI
920-854-2900

*Maple Grove Motel
809 Hwy 42
Gills Rock, WI
920-854-2587

*Village View Inn
10628 Bayshore Dr
Sister Bay, WI
920-854-2813

*Ephraim Motel
10407 Hwy 42
Sister Bay, WI
920-854-5959

*Main Street Motel
4209 Main St
Fish Creek, WI
920-868-2201

*The Shallows Resort
7353 Horseshoe Bay Rd
Egg Harbor, WI
920-868-3458

Best Western Inn
1001 N 14th Ave
Sturgeon Bay, WI
920-743-7231

Chadwick Inn
25 N 8th Ave
Sturgeon Bay, WI
920-743-2771

Stone Harbor Resort
107 N 5th Ave
Sturgeon Bay, WI
920-746-0700

Super 8 Motel
409 Green Bay Rd
Sturgeon Bay, WI
920-743-9211
(across the bridge)

Bike Shops

*Nor Door Sport & Cyclery
4007 Hwy 42
Fish Creek, WI
920-868-2275

Nor Door Sport & Cyclery
60 Madison Ave
Sturgeion Bay, WI
920-818-0803

Ellison Bay to Sturgeon Bay (70 Miles)

Miles N/S	Directions	Dist	R	Service	Miles S/N
0	S at SS to cross SH 42 on Cedar Shore Rd (*Ellison Bay)	0.3	3	GLQR	70
0	L at SS on Garrett Bay Rd	2.8	3		70
3	R at SS on Garrett Bay Hill Rd	0.2	3		67
3	L at SS on Cottage Rd	1.1	3		67
	*Gills Rock			LR	
4	VL at SS on SH 42	2.4	3	L	66
	*Ferry				
7	S on SH 42	2.4	3		63
9	R on Cottage Rd	1.1	3		61
10	R on Garrett Bay Hill Rd	0.2	3		60
10	L on Garrett Bay Rd	2.8	3		60
13	R on Cedar Shore Rd	0.3	3		57
	*Ellison Bay			GLQR	
13	R on SH 42	5.6	3	CL	56
	*Sister Bay			GLQR	
19	Continue S on SH 42	3.8	3		51
	*Ephraim			GLQR	
23	Continue S on SH 42	1.2	3		47
24	R on Shore Rd	8.0	1	C	46
32	R at SS on SH 42	0.4	3		38
32	S on Main St (*Fish Creek)	0.1	3	LR	37
33	L at SS on Cottage Row	1.6	3		37
34	R on Gibralter Bluff Rd	1.4	3		36
36	L at SS on Pennsula Player Rd	0.4	3		34
36	R at SS on Egg Harbor Rd/SH 42	0.6	3		34
37	R on Juddville Rd	0.4	3		33
37	L on White Cliff Rd	3.2	3		33
40	S on Dock Rd	0.2	2		30
	*Egg Harbor			CGLQR	
40	R at SS on CR G/Horseshoe Bay Rd	3.7	3		30
44	VR on CR B/Bay Shore Dr (as CR G turns left)	13.7	3	CL	26
58	S on N 3rd Ave/ CR B (*Sturgeon Bay)	0.8	3	GLQR	12
59	R on Michigan St/Madison Ave	0.5	3		11
59	R at SL on Maple St	0.6	3		11

60	R at SS on Duluth Ave/ CR C	0.5	3		10
60	L at SS CR C	1.4	3		10
62	R on Park Dr	1.0	3	C	8
63	L on Sand Bay Rd	4.5	3	C	7
67	VL on Wood Lane Rd	0.5	3	R	3
68	L on Stevenson's Pier Rd	2.3	3	CL	2
70	R at SS on CR C		3	QR	0

Beautifully preserved Eagle Bluff Lighthouse within Peninsula State Park.

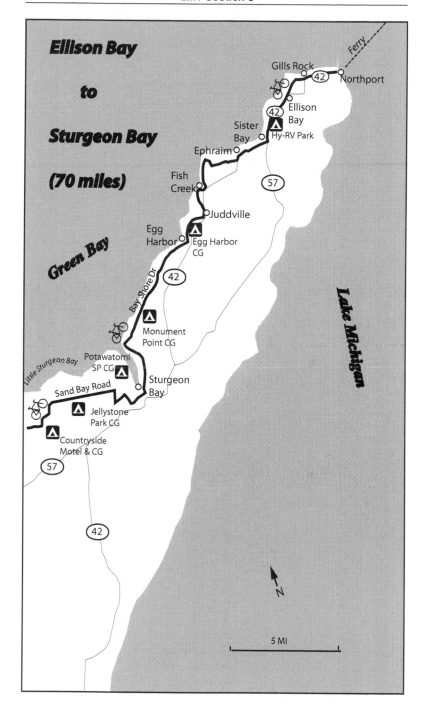

Ellison Bay

to

Sturgeon Bay

(70 miles)

Green Bay

Gills Rock
Northport
42
Ferry
Ellison Bay
42
Sister Bay
Hy-RV Park
Ephraim
57
Fish Creek
Juddville
Egg Harbor
Egg Harbor CG
Bay Shore Dr
42
Monument Point CG
Potawatomi SP CG
Little Sturgeon Bay
Sturgeon Bay
Sand Bay Road
Jellystone Park CG
Countryside Motel & CG
57
42
Lake Michigan
N
5 Mi

Lake Michigan Trail
OPTIONAL TOUR

Washington Island (22 miles)

This isn't officially part of the LMT, but it's a nice side trip, plus you get to ride another ferry. It's only about a thirty minute boat ride, but it offers some great views of the shores of both the mainland and the islands you pass on the crossing. If you enjoy ferries like I do, you have the option to take another ferry on the other side of Washington Island that will take you to Rock Island. More on Rock Island later.

If you are paying for your trip using plastic and you are also planning to visit Rock Island, you will need to buy both ferry tickets at the Northport Car Ferry booth. As of the time of this printing, the Rock Island Ferry did not take credit cards.

The price of the round trip Washington Island Ferry is $13.50 for an adult, plus $4.00 for a bike. The cost for the Rock Island Ferry is $11.00 for an adult, plus $3.00 for a cart. The combination ticket for an adult round trip for both islands is $24.

Prior to today's modern navigation tools, the passage the ferry takes between the mainland and this group of islands was pretty treacherous, so perilous in fact that early French explorers referred to it as "Porte des Morte", which translates to the "Door of Death". The origin of the name goes back to 1850, when several canoes filled with Potawatomi Native Americans crashed their boats into the rocky bluffs of one of the islands. However, as the story goes, most of the warriors were actually killed by a welcome party of Winnebago warriors who finished off the survivors. But I'll let the locals fill in the remainder of that story.

The passage continued to live up to its name for early European ships also. An example would be the fall of 1870, when over 100 large vessels were stranded or damaged passing through the "Door".

There are over one hundred miles of paved roads on Washington Island, however dead end roads leading to the shoreline and parallel roads crisscrossing the island multiple times account for most of those miles, so don't worry, you won't have to ride all one hundred miles when touring the island. The routes selected in the guidebook were based on Wisconsin coastal guide recommendations. These are bike-friendly roads that route cyclists past many interesting areas, such as Jackson Harbor, Dunes Park, Detroit Harbor Natural Area, and other attractions that make this side trip so inviting.

However, with the island's high bluffs and rocky shores, there are some fantastic views to be found if you have the time to ride some of the dead end roads leading to the island's shore. When you stop to collect literature and maps at the Welcome Center on Lobdell Point Road, which is located very near where the ferry docked, ask them to suggest the best side roads to take for the best views. The ones I took were nice, but I wasn't able to check out every one of them, so the Welcome Center would be a better source for information.

Less than two miles into your ride on County Road W, which begins as Lobdell Point Road, you will intersect with Main Road. A lot of the businesses on the island are located in this general area. Several of the lodgings listed in the guidebook are in this area. There are several eating establishments here also. Less than two miles further into the loop on Main Road you pass Mann's Store, a full service grocery and deli.

As you are following the loop described in the Mileage Log and reach the end of Jackson Harbor Road, if you are interested in visiting Rock Island, continue left for less than a mile to reach the ferry landing. The Jackson Harbor Inn, listed in the guidebook, is located at the ferry landing in case you need a place to stay before embarking on your Rock Island adventure.

Rock Island is an interesting place to visit but it is pretty primitive. The entire island is a state park. There are no stores on the island, so be sure to take all your supplies. Drinking water is available near the dock and boathouse. There are also vault toilets.

You are allowed to take your bike to the island; however you are not allowed to ride it on the island. I guess that's why the description of the ferry rates specifies "cart', rather than bicycle. You are basically using your bike as a cart to haul your gear to camp. It beats having to leave your bike on Washington Island and schlep your equipment around the island by hand.

If you include a trip to Rock Island, be sure to visit the Potowatomi Lighthouse. It was the first United States commissioned lighthouse on Lake Michigan. The lighthouse has been completely refurbished and is open to the public for tours.

There are ten miles of trails on the island and six miles of shoreline for hiking. It is strongly recommended that you reserve a campsite ahead of your visit by calling 888-947-2757.

Be sure to take plenty of warm clothing. With the lake water temperatures only in the high 30s the onshore breezes keep the island pretty cool.

When you stop at the Welcome Center on Washington Island at the beginning of your tour, you will collect information for various attractions on the island; however there are a couple that I want to point out.

Embarking on ferry ride across the "Door of Death".

72

The Jackson Harbor Maritime Museum is one of these places. It is located on the County Road W loop, on Jackson Harbor Road, making it a convenient place to stop for a break.

The Mountain Park and Lookout Tower, located on Mountain Road, is another place I recommend. This is a worthwhile stop because after climbing up the 186 steps to the top of the tower you have a beautiful view of the surrounding island and water.

The Potowatomi Native Americans were the first known residents of this island grouping on Lake Michigan. They were here to greet the first immigrants to arrive as they came from Finland, Ireland, Norway, Denmark, Iceland, and Sweden. The Scandinavian flavor of these early settlers is prevalent to this day, with Washington Island being the second largest Icelandic community in North America. Thumb through a local telephone directory to find names like Gunnlaugsson, Bjarnarson, and Jorgenson, and see that the descendants of the early settlers continue to inhabit the island.

The ride around Washington Island is a pleasant experience. The roads route you through a lot of ever green forests and across rural countryside, plus there isn't much traffic. I thought the Door Peninsula was isolated and remote, but in comparison, the ride around this place makes that look like downtown Chicago.

Camping

Washington CG	Rock Island SP
745 Eastside Rd	1924 Indian Point Rd
Washington Island, WI	Rock Island, WI
920-847-2622	920-847-2235

Lodging

Findlay's Holiday Inn	*Frog Hollow Farm B&B	Jackson Harbor Inn
1860 The Inn Rd	1029 Jackson Harbor Rd	1899 Jackson Harbor Rd
Washington Island, WI	Rock Island, WI	Rock Island, WI
800-522-5469	920-847-2835	920-847-2454
Cedar Point Inn	Gibson's West Harbor Resort	Viking Village Motel
2119 Green Bay Rd	2206 West Harbor Rd	735 Main Rd
Washington Island, WI	Rock Island, WI	Rock Island, WI
920-847-2180	920-847-2225	920-847-2551

Bike Shops

N/A

Washington Island (22 Miles)

Miles N/S	Directions	Dist	R	Service	Miles S/N
	*Washington Island Ferry				
0	S on Lobdell Rd	1.7	2		22
2	L at SS on Main Rd	2.6	2	GR	20
4	R on Jackson Harbor Rd	3.5	2		18
8	S on Old Camp Rd	0.6	2		14
8	R on Old Camp Rd	0.1	2		14
9	S on Sunrise Dr	1.1	2		14
10	R on Town Line Rd	2.0	2		13
12	L on East Side Rd	1.0	2		11
13	L on Lake View Rd	1.1	3		10
14	L on Hemlock Dr	2.7	3		8
16	S across Woodland Rd on Shore Rd	2.5	3		6
19	S on Range Line Rd	0.3	4		3
19	L on Homestead Ln	0.2	3		3
19	VR on Detroit Harbor Rd	1.0	2		3
20	S on Lobdell Rd	1.7	2		2
22	*Washington Island Ferry				0

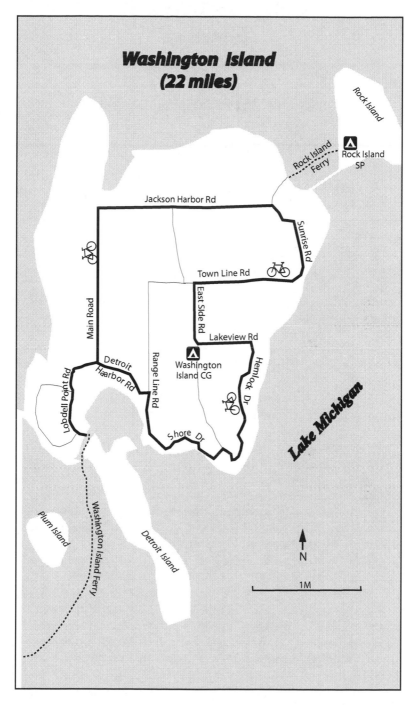

Washington Island
(22 miles)

Rock Island

Rock Island Ferry

Rock Island SP

Jackson Harbor Rd

Sunrise Rd

Town Line Rd

Main Road

East Side Rd

Lakeview Rd

Washington Island CG

Detroit Harbor Rd

Range Line Rd

Hemlock Dr

Lobdell Point Rd

Shore Dr

Lake Michigan

Plum Island

Washington Island Ferry

Detroit Island

N

1M

Lake Michigan Trail
SECTION 10

Sturgeon Bay to Oconto (70 miles)

It was odd preparing the map for this section and not having Lake Michigan in it. For this section, the LMT borders Green Bay, 120 miles long and over 20 miles wide.

When you look at Green Bay on a map you see that it is almost cut off from Lake Michigan. The Door Peninsula stretches out across the mouth of the bay from the south, the Garden Peninsula drops down from Michigan's Upper Peninsula, and a string of islands scattered across the remainder of the opening nearly form a solid bay-mouth barrier. The long escarpment creating the land mass that almost encloses the bay is part of the same formation that creates the cliffs of Niagara Falls. Ponder that as you are pedaling some of the open stretches of highways included in this section. Also, think about how if there had been a ferry at Newport for the 20 some miles across to the mainland of the Upper Peninsula, you could have eliminated the 200-plus-mile ride around the bay. But, then think of all the great touring you would have missed.

As you are riding through the beginning of this section watch for produce stands along the highway to pick up some locally grown fruit the area is known for. It's always nice to eat food that may have been picked that same day, plus it's good to support the independent farmers.

The scenery while riding along 4 Corners Road reminded me of some of the wetlands I passed on the MRT in Louisiana's Bayou Country. It's mentally therapeutic to ride past these small bodies of water alongside the road, thick with vegetation, and get glimpses of waterfowl foraging naturally for foodstuff.

The Red River Park you pass along here has picnic tables, restrooms, and a small beach, but camping is not allowed.

When riding Sturgeon Road and you turn onto Rockfalls Road, just ignore the "Road Closed" sign. They're not talking about us. Automobiles will have to turn around but bicycles will continue on a separated bike trail. I was so relieved when I discovered this paved trail. I thought I was going to have to ride on a very busy stretch of State Highway 57.

As an added bonus, the bike trail drops you off at Bay Shore

76

Campground. Sweet! If you are not ready to camp, there are also picnic tables and restrooms to take a break. When leaving the camping area, once again just prior to reaching State Highway 57, you take a lesser road off to your right.

I was originally going to rate Nicolet Drive a 3, because even though the road has a good shoulder I felt the traffic might be heavy at times. However, I met a group of local cyclists through here and they bragged that this was one of the best rides in the Green Bay area. Who am I to argue, I gave it a 2.

You pass a historic monument along Nicolet Drive commemorating the location where Jean Nicolet, an emissary of New France, landed in 1634. You also begin to see the skyline of Green Bay up ahead, so get out your Packer's cycling jersey. I'm a big Green Bay Packer fan, just like I'm a fan of the hometown team for any place I'm cycling through. It doesn't hurt, and sometimes it has its perks. When my touring bud, Bob Cable, and I were riding the MRT in southern Louisiana, we stopped in a small town at the Chamber of Commerce to ask if there were any parks or other areas where we could pitch our tents. One of the guys working there asked if we were LSU fans. I quickly responded, "They're one of my favorite teams." It turns out LSU was playing Texas in football that evening. The guy owned some rental cottages, and he happened to have one that was between renters. So he let Bob and I stay there, and he even hooked up the television cable for us so we could watch the game. So, I always cheer for the local team.

Speaking of the Packers, if you would like to collect more information about the Green Bay area to help you plan your trip, the Visitor Bureau is located right across from Lambeau Field, at 1901 South Oneida Street. While you are in that neighborhood, visit the "Walk of Legends" walkway to see just how devoted Packer fans are to their team. The walkway is lined by 24, 12-ton, 14-foot tributes that chronicle the evolution of football in Green Bay. Pretty impressive!

The city's downtown is divided into three districts. After crossing the East River you enter the Downtown District. This is the locale to be in during the evening for dining, theatre, and pubs. If you turn left on Main Street, instead of crossing the bridge across Fox River, you enter the Olde Main Street District. Here you will find arts, ethnic grocery stores, and restaurants. Then, after crossing the Fox River Bridge you will be in the On Broadway District. This area is known for its eclectic shops, brewpubs, dining, and a very impressive Farmers Market. If you stay at the Clarion

Hotel, located alongside the East River Trail, all of the districts will be readily accessible.

The traffic gets pretty busy after crossing the Fox River Bridge. There is a sidewalk along Military Avenue you might want to take advantage of. When reaching Bond Street traffic lets up a little, and then picks back up again on Velp Avenue. I was advised to include the brief zag off of Velp Avenue to avoid the busiest section. The AmericInn lodging listed on Velp Avenue is just beyond the turn onto Riverview Drive. When you return to Velp Avenue you are out of town but still not out of the traffic right away. Beginning at Riverside Drive you finally leave the 'burbs behind and you're back in farm country. As a matter of fact, you ride past a "Land of Lakes" farm, the people who make the butter I eat at home.

After riding in the city for a while it's nice to get back out on a country road again. The long stretches of highways that take you to the end of this section are pretty much tree-lined open roads that are off the beaten path. To reach the restaurant listed for Little Suamico you will need to ride a couple of miles west on County Road S, and even after this detour it is only a pizza parlor.

Upon reaching Oconto you will have your choice of places to eat and sleep. This is a full service town, including camping. Oconto is another nice community to tour on a bicycle; they even encourage visitors to tour via bicycle with their "Ride Oconto History" campaign. It is great to visit a small town and see all the downtown buildings occupied. The Beyer Home Museum makes for an enjoyable stop to stretch your legs and learn more about the history of the area.

Camping

*Bay Shore Park CG	Oconto City Park CG	Holtwood CG
5637 Hwy 57	5182 County Hwy N	400 Holtwood Way
New Franken, WI	Oconto, WI	Oconto, Wi
920-448-6242	920-834-7706	920-834-7732

Lodging

Smith's Shoreline Cottages	Sunset Beach Motel	*Clarion Hotel
9250 Lime Liln Rd	N8931 Hwy 57	201 Main St
Sturgeon, WI	Dyckesville, WI	Green Bay, WI
920-493-1610	920-866-2978	920-437-5900
(2 miles off CR C)		

Motel 6
1614 Shawano Ave
Green Bay, WI
920-494-6730

*AmericInn Suites
2032 Velp Ave
Green Bay, WI
920-434-9790

Riverview Inn & Suites
600 Brazeau Ave
Oconto, WI
920-834-5559

Bike Shops

In Competition Sports
2439 University Ave
Green Bay, WI
920-465-6067

JB Cycle & Sport Inc
2500 Glendale Ave
Green Bay, WI
920-434-8338
(less than 1 mile off LMT)

Stadium Bike
2150 Mason St
Green Bay, WI
920-499-3400

A pair of lovely ladies I met on the road. They didn't have much to say, but they were good listeners.

Sturgeon Bay to Oconto (70 miles)

Miles N/S	Directions	Dist	R	Service	Miles S/N
0	R at SS on CR C	3.5	3	QR	70
4	L at SS on CR C/Circle Ridge Rd	2.5	3		66
6	R on 4 Corners Rd/CR N	5.6	3		64
12	R at SS on CR DK	8.0	3	LQR	58
	*Dyckesville			R	50
20	VR on Sturgeon Rd/CR DK	0.9	3		50
20	R on Rockfalls Rd	0.5	1		49
21	S on Bike Path	0.9	P	C	49
22	L on Bayshore Rd	0.3	1		48
22	R on Sunset Bluff Dr	1.3	3	QR	48
23	R at SS on Nicolet Dr	8.9	2	R	46
32	R on East Shore Dr	2.2	3		37
35	R at SS on Irving Ave then VL on Bay Beach Rd	0.8	3		35
35	L on Quincy St	1.3	3		34
37	R at SL University AVE/SH 57 to cross East River	0.1	3		33
37	R on East River Tr after crossing bridge	0.9	P		33
	*Green Bay			GLQR	32
38	L on ramp then R on Main St/Dousman St Bridge to cross Fox River	2.3	4		32
40	R at SL on Military Ave	0.4	4		30
40	L at SL on Bond St	0.7	3		29
41	R at SS on Taylor St	0.2	3		29
41	L on Vincent RD	0.4	3		28
42	R at SS on Memorial Dr	0.8	3		28
42	L at SS on Velp Ave/CR HS	0.3	5	LR	27
43	R at SL on Riverview Dr	0.3	3	QR	27
43	L on Glendale Ave	0.6	3		27
44	R at SL on Velp Ave	4.7	3	GQR	26
48	R on Riverside Dr	0.8	3	R	21
	*Suamico			GQR	21
49	L at SS on Lakeview Dr/CR J	6.5	3		21
	*Little Suamico				
56	R on CR S	14.0	3	R	14
70	R at SS on Main St/CR Y (*Oconto)		3	CGLQR	0

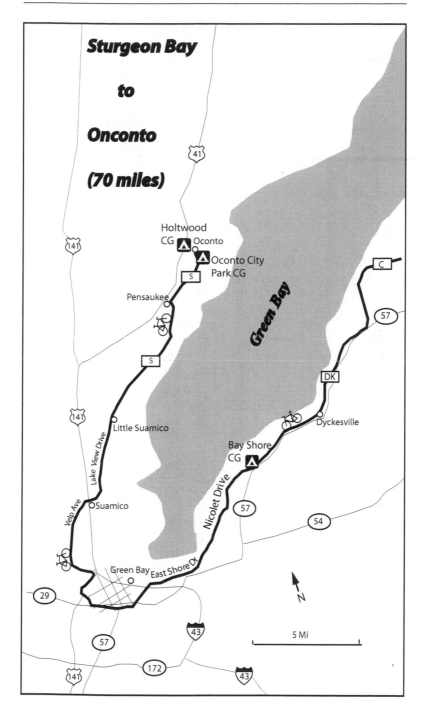

Lake Michigan Trail
SECTION 11

Oconto to Escanaba (79 miles)

This is the last section of our ride that follows the Green Bay shoreline. You will be back on Lake Michigan in the next section, as you ride across Michigan's Upper Peninsula. There are several camping opportunities in this section. The first one you encounter is located about 9 miles north of Oconto. Turn right off of the LMT onto Bay Road, and after less than a mile's ride you will reach the North Bay Shore Recreation Area Campground.

On your ride through Peshtigo stop to visit the Peshtigo Fire Museum, located at 400 Oconto Avenue. Fire destroyed all but one building in town, so there aren't many artifacts remaining for display. It is an interesting stop none the less, as you read firsthand accounts of the event and see dramatic before and after photos of the town. The fire occurred October 8th, 1871, the same day as the Great Chicago Fire, the Holland, Michigan Fire, the Port Huron Fire, and the Great Michigan Fire in Manistee, Michigan. However, with an estimated 1,200 to 2,500 deaths and over 1.5 million acres of charred land, the Peshtigo Fire is considered to be the deadliest in American history.

Also visit the Peshtigo Cemetery, which is adjacent to the museum. You can pay your respects at the mass grave where 300 unidentified bodies were buried, along with the gravesites of many other fire victims.

There were two different names on street signs for Old Peshtigo Road when I rode through. Don't get confused or frustrated when you see this, just ignore the sign when they call it another name and you will soon see a sign calling it Old Peshtigo Road once again.

To reach the Marinette Comfort Inn, listed in the guidebook, turn left at the Roosevelt Road crossing. The inn is conveniently located only a tenth of a mile from the intersection.

Use caution at the railroad crossing on State Street in the town of Marinette. Shortly after crossing these rough tracks, plan to stop for lunch at the Blue Bike Burrito, on Hall Avenue. Owner John LaPlant uses locally grown organic ingredients and hand cut meats to provide his patrons the freshest, best tasting meal possible. The meal is prepared right in front of you, so as a bonus, the price of your meal includes entertainment. BTW, the blue bike in the name is in reference to a bicycle, not a motorcycle, so you gotta support this place.

As you cross the Menominee River on the Bridge Street Bridge, you are also crossing the state line into Michigan. If you peer to your right, just after the river crossing, you can see the River Park Campground. Although the campground is only a few feet away from the bridge, to reach the entrance you have to continue to follow the LMT another half a mile to the intersection of 10th Avenue and 10th Street. Here, you leave the LMT by turning right on 10th Street and riding another half a mile.

You pass the Menominee lodging that is listed in the guidebook shortly after turning left at the intersection of 10th Avenue and 10th Street. I know it's confusing having 10th intersecting with 10th, but I'm sure there was a logical explanation for doing this. You will also have opportunities to stock up on supplies along State Highway 41, before embarking on the long ride along State Highway 35.

Traffic remains heavy as you exit Menominee on State Highway 35, but eventually it lets up. Occasionally there will be views of the waters of Green Bay in between homes, and on a clear day you can see all the way across the bay to its eastern shore.

There are several parks to stop in for a break along the highway. Bailey's Park is one of the parks you pass, which is also the location for the West Shore Fishing Museum. The museum is a restored late 1800s commercial fishery that includes several buildings and exhibits associated with commercial fishing of that era. When I rode through the museum was only opened to the public on weekends.

I like that State Highway 35 has the rumble strips in the center of the highway rather than on the shoulder. It makes more sense to me to warn people of a possible head on collusion rather than when they drift off the road onto the shoulder. When it is in the center it also means the entire shoulder is available for bicycles.

There is nothing complicated about touring Michigan's Upper Peninsula. It's just wide open roads through lush forest, over easy rolling hills, alongside lakes and streams. An added bonus is that there are not a lot of turns to remember.

About 3 miles south of Escanaba the LMT passes a turn for the Portage Marsh Wildlife Viewing area. It is a little over a 1 mile ride to reach the site. The viewing locale includes several social trails through various types of wetland habitat, and an elevated foot-path that is ideal for wildlife viewing. The marsh is a popular stopover for migrating water fowl during the months of April and October.

Traffic can be busy in Escanaba, so take advantage of the separated paved path paralleling US Highway 2. When the path runs out you can then ride the service road. Also, watch for traffic turning into the numerous businesses along the highway.

Camping

*North Bay Shore CG
Bay Rd
Peshtigo, WI
(just off Cty Rd Y)

Badger Park CG & Cabins
W Park Dr
Peshtigo, WI
715-582-4321

*Kleinke Park CG
Hwy 35
Menominee, MI
906-753-4582

*JW Wells SP
N 7670 Hwy 35
Cedar River, MI
906-863-9747

*Fox Park CG
Hwy 35
Cedar River, MI
(6 miles north of Cedar River)

*Park Place of the North CG
E4575 Hwy 35
Escanaba, MI
906-786-8453

Lodging

Ramada Inn
600 Brazeau Ave
Oconto, WI
920-834-5559

*Edgewater Motel
790 French St
Peshtigo, WI
715-582-4559

*Comfort Inn
2180 Roosevelt Rd
Marinette, WI
715-732-2321

Best Western Riverside Inn
1821 Riverside Ave
Marinette, WI
715-732-1000

*AmericInn
2330 10th St
Menominee, MI
906-863-8190

*Econo Lodge
2516 10th St
Menominee, MI
906-863-4431

*Riverview Inn
M8212 Hwy 35
Cedar River, MI
906-864-0014

Best Western Inn
2635 Ludington St
Escanaba, MI
906-786-0602

Comfort Suites
3600 Ludington St
Escanaba, MI
906-786-9630

Bike Shops

Marinette Cycle Center
1555 Pierce Ave
Marinette, WI
715-735-5442

Cyclepath
2329 13th St
Menominee, MI
906-863-9361

Mr Bike Ski & Fitness
1016 Ludinton St
Escanaba, MI
906-786-1200

Oconto to Escanabe (79 miles)

Miles N/S	Directions	Dist	R	Service	Miles S/N
0	*Oconto			CGLQR	
0	R at SS on Main St/CR Y	13.4	3	C	79
	*Peshtigo (ride over US 41)			CGLQR	
13	VR on French St/US 41B	1.2	3		66
15	VR on Front St/US 41B	0.1	2		64
16	L on Maple St/US 41B	1.5	3		63
16	S on Schacht Rd/US 41B (under US 41)	0.2	4	R	63
16	L on Old Peshtigo Rd	3.4	3	R	63
20	S at SS on Woleske Rd	1.1	3	LQR	59
21	L on Industrial Pkwy	0.3	3		58
21	R at SS on Cleveland Ave	0.1	3		58
21	L on Industrial Pkwy	0.2	3		58
21	R at SS on Mary St	0.1	3		58
21	L on Ridge St	0.2	3		58
22	R at SS on Carney Ave	0.1	3		57
22	L on State St	0.3	3		57
22	VR on Hattie St	0.2	3		57
22	R at SL on Hall Ave	0.3	3		57
	(*Marinette)			GLQR	
23	VL at SL on Bridge St	0.8	2		57
23	VR on 10th Ave	0.3	4		56
	*Menominee			GLQR	
24	L at SL on 10 St/US 41	1.8	5	LQR	55
25	R at SL on SH 35	23.6	3	C	54
	*Cedar River			GLQR	
49	S on SH 35	23.4	3	C	30
	*Ford River			GLR	
72	S on SH 35	6.6	3	C	7
79	*Escanaba			GLQR	0

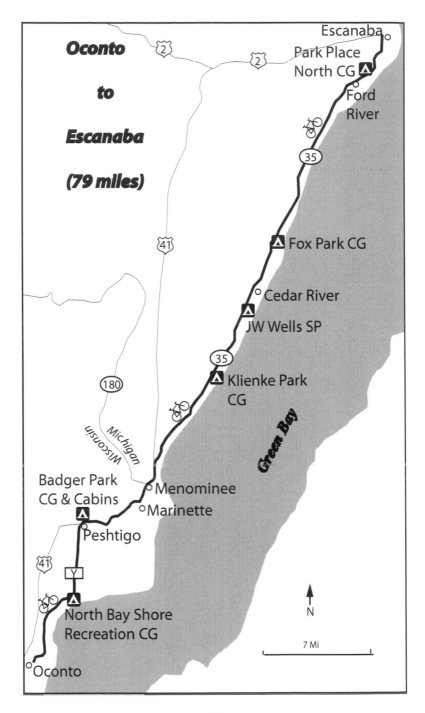

Oconto

to

Escanaba

(79 miles)

Escanaba

Park Place
North CG

Ford
River

35

Fox Park CG

Cedar River

JW Wells SP

35

Klienke Park
CG

Green Bay

Badger Park
CG & Cabins

Menominee

Marinette

Peshtigo

41

North Bay Shore
Recreation CG

Oconto

N

7 Mi

Wisconsin

Michigan

Lake Michigan Trail
SECTION 12

Escanaba to Gulliver (75 miles)

In the town of Gladstone, the LMT routes cyclists off of busy US 2 onto side roads that take you through the old downtown area. Immediately after exiting US 2 onto Lake Shore Drive, you pass Van Cleve Park, which has restrooms, picnic tables, and a swimming beach. Following this, on 9th Street, you pass Four J's Family Restaurant, which serves reasonably priced traditional home cooked meals.

There are some long stretches in this section where there are not a lot of lodging or dining options, however, as for camping, you will find several places to pitch a tent. Plus, you can always pull off on a gravel road in the Hiawatha National Forest to stealth camp among the pine trees. As I said earlier, I'm not advocating camping without permission, so I only mention this for those touring cyclists who partake in the practice.

I passed an interesting old garage in Rapid River that had collected a lot of unusual artifacts outside the building. I thought it might make for an interesting visit, but there was no one available when I stopped. If anyone stops and visits with the owner let me know the story behind the relics they have assembled.

A little over 2 miles east of Rapid River on US 2, you can take a 5 mile ride off the LMT on County Road 513 to reach the Little Bay de Noc Campground. Each site is located on the shore of the bay, and there is a swimming beach and hiking trail.

Although US 2 has high speed limits, it isn't a bad road to ride. There are wide shoulders on most of it, and there aren't a lot of sharp turns to block a motorist's view.

There are several attractions to visit along this section of the LMT; however most of them involve a side trip. If you are in a hurry, just continue to follow the primary LMT route across the Upper Peninsula. However, if you have the time to ride a few extra miles, venture off-route and explore the areas I will describe.

One such side trip is the community of Nahma. This is an historic area that had once been a booming lumber and sawmill town in the late 1800s. After exhausting the area timber, the mill shutdown and the residents began to leave. Finally the entire town was put up for sale in 1951. The sale made national news when it was featured in a story in Life Magazine. Today there is a small general store, a museum, the Upper Peninsula Resort (which has cabins and camping,906-644-2728), and a very nice inn. A stay at the Nahma Inn alone is worth the 5 mile ride each way. It is a quaint lodge with a restaurant and lounge. Unless I was planning to stay at the inn, I personally don't think I would make the ride again. But, if you don't mind adding a few miles and you have the time, it is a nice little town to visit. Follow County Road Gg to reach Nahma. The turn for this road is about 9 miles east of the town of Ensign on US 2.

Twin blast furnaces at historic Fayette State Park.

Another side trip that I do recommend, even if you do not plan to spend the night, is Fayette State Park. You have to ride 17 miles, each way, on State Highway 183, but it is an interesting place to visit. The park itself is a reconstructed industrial community that manufactured pig iron from 1867 to 1891. It is a living museum with still ongoing reclamation. Walk through the 20 standing buildings to learn firsthand what life was like when the community was home to over 500 residents. Many of the buildings have informational displays describing that building's purpose in the community. There is also a loading dock on Snail Shell Harbor that was used to export pig iron by ship. FYI, the harbor is now available for boat camping, something for me to remember when I tour Lake Michigan by boat next time.

The state park has a campground, the Furnace Hill Lodge, and a visitor center. Just past the entrance to the park is Sherry's Port Bar, a friendly place to grab a bite to eat and have a beer. You can also stop in the town of Garden, located between US 2 and the state park, where you will find a motel and café. Like I said, I think this side trip is definitely worth the extra miles.

When I noticed that I was riding through Schoolcraft County I checked to see if it was named after the same Schoolcraft I kept hearing about when I was researching the Bicycling Guide to the Mississippi River Trail. Yes, this was the same Henry Rowe Schoolcraft who explored the source of the Mississippi River in Minnesota. Wow, some people have really left behind a lasting legacy.

The LMT passes a Visitor Information Center as you enter the town of Manistique, if you would like to check out the local attractions and spend some time in the area. It also passes the Mackinaw Trail Winery, for a convenient stop to sample a few of the local wines.

Just after crossing the Manistique River you might notice a separated paved path off to your right. This is a short trail that runs through a park with restrooms; however there is a sign stating that bicycles are not allowed on the path. Weird?

The LMT passes several motels on the ride through Manistique and presents a variety of options to eat. You might also want to pick up some snacks for the road, because once you leave town there are no services for the remainder of this section. There are also no immediate services in Gulliver, at the end of this section.

After exiting Manistique the LMT leaves US 2 for a while, taking advantage of lesser traveled county roads. If you prefer, you can remain on US 2 because the LMT rejoins it later. However, the LMT route is only about a mile longer than if you remain on US 2. If you are only taking the River Road route to reach Merwin Creek State Forest Campground, later in this section I will point out an option just past the campground to return to US 2 earlier than the LMT route does. It's great to have options.

There was a convenience store at the turn for River Road, but it was shut down when I came through. Traffic was low on River Road. It doesn't offer much in the way of scenery, just your typical county road, but it was a welcome break from US 2. About 5 miles into the ride you pass the turn for the Merwin Creek State Forest Campground. The campground is a little over a mile off route. The camp sites are primitive; however there are vault toilets and potable water.

As I mentioned earlier, if you are in a hurry to return to US 2, when River Road reaches a T-intersection with County Road 438, when the LMT turns left, you can turn right and return to US 2.

Although there are no services at the intersection where the LMT returns to US 2, about 4 miles after turning left on US 2 you reach the Dreamland Motel & Restaurant. This is a nice family operation and the restaurant serves up some really tasty food.

Camping

*Pioneer Trail Park CG	Little Bay De Noc CG	*Whispering Valley RV CG
6822 US 2	5 miles on CR 513	8410 US 2
Gladstone, MI	Rapid River, MI	Rapid River, MI
906-786-1020	877-444-6777	906-474-7044
Fayette State Park CG	Indian Lake SP	*Merwin Creek SF CG
4785 II Rd (Hwy 183)	8970 W CR 442	Merwin Rd
Garden, MI	Manistique, MI	Gulliver, MI
906-644-2603	906-341-2355	906-341-3618
	(3 miles on Hwy 149)	(1 mile off LMT)

Lodging

*Gladstone Motel	*Shorewood Motel	*Hill Crest Motel
101 S 9th St	1226 N Lakeshore Dr	10154 US 2
Gladstone, MI	Gladstone, MI	Rapid River, MI
906-661-3438	906-428-9624	906-474-6696

Nahma Inn
13747 Main St
Nahma, MI
906-644-2486

Tyelene's Motel
16086 Old US 2
Cooks, Mi
906-644-7163

Garden Bay Motel
9107 Oo 25 Rd
Garden, Mi
906-644-2258

Furnace Hill Lodge
Hwy 183 (Fayette SP)
Garden, MI
906-644-2603

*North Shore Motel
801 E Lakeshore Dr
Manistique, Mi
906-341-4151

*Comfort Inn
617 E Lakeshore DR
Manistique, MI
906-341-6981

Bike Shops

Brampton Bike & Ski
910 Delta Ave
Gladstone,. MI
906-428-2135

Escanabe to Gulliver (75 miles)

Miles N/S	Directions	Dist	R	Service	Miles S/N
	*Escanaba				75
0	S at SL on US 2/US 41	7.7	3	C	75
	*Gladstone			GLQR	68
8	VR on Lake Shore Dr	1.2	3	QR	68
9	VL on 9th St	1.2	3	LQR	67
10	VR on Lake Shore Dr/Bay Shore Dr	3.7	3	LQR	65
14	R on 6 Rd/ CRI-39	0.4	2		62
14	VL on S 75 Rd/CRI-39	1.1	3		61
15	R at SS on Bay Shore Rd	0.1	3		60
	*Rapid River			LQR	60
15	R at SS on US 2	6.3	3	CLQR	60
	*Ensign				54
22	S on US 2	19.5	3	LQ	54
	*Cooks			LR	34
41	S on US 2	15.5	3	LR	34
57	S on US 2	3.8	3	CGLQR	19
	*Manistique			GLQR	15
61	L on River Rd/CR 433	6.0	3	C	15
67	L at SS on River Rd/CR 433	3.5	3		9
70	R on River Rd/Quarry Rd/CR 433	5.4	3		5
75	L at SS on US 2		3	LQ	0
	*Gulliver				

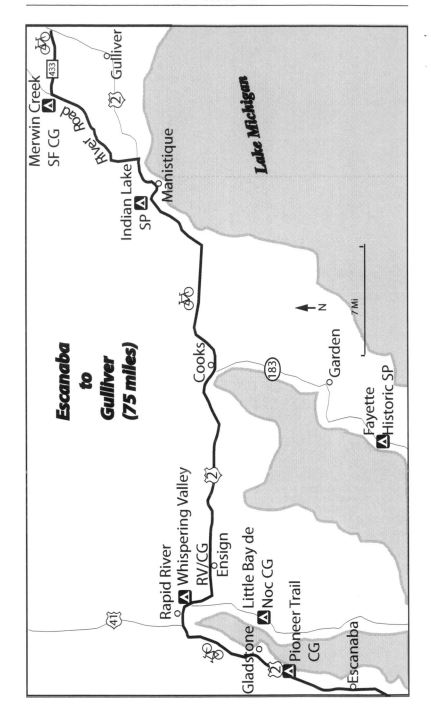

Escanaba
to
Gulliver
(75 miles)

Lake Michigan

Gulliver
Merwin Creek SF CG
River Road
Manistique
Indian Lake SP
Cooks
Garden
Fayette Historic SP
N
7 Mi
Whispering Valley RV/CG
Rapid River
Ensign
Little Bay de Noc CG
Pioneer Trail CG
Gladstone
Escanaba

Lake Michigan Trail
SECTION 13

Gulliver to St. Ignace (72 miles)

In this section, as with the previous section, you are riding in an eastward direction, so the map is displayed landscape in order to better fit the page. Once again, there are some long stretches of open highway in the segment, but the area has been serving tourists' needs for a number of years, so you will have plenty of choices for lodging, eating, and camping. Services are not limited to within city limits either. Many of the lodging and restaurant establishments are scattered along the highway between townships. As for camping, there are too many camping opportunities to include all of them in the guidebook. The ones I have listed are spaced along the section for you to better plan your daily mileage, however, be assured there are plenty of additional campgrounds.

One of the first campgrounds you encounter is the Milakokia Lake State Forest Campground. You pass the right turn onto Milakokia Lake Road about 9 miles into this section. The campground is on this road about 3 miles off-route. The sites are rustic; however there are vault toilets and potable water.

If you prefer to avoid riding additional miles off the LMT route to reach a campsite, continue along US 2 another 7 miles to reach Michihistrian Bar-Campground and Cabins. The business is situated right alongside the highway, and there is also a restaurant.

The Hog Island Country Store and Cottages has been catering to the needs of visitors to the Upper Peninsula since the 1940s. The building housing the store dates back even further, to 1914, when it was used as a cabin at a nearby lumber camp. Stop by to explore the interesting artifacts the owners have collected over the years and also to purchase snacks of homemade jams, jellies, and smoked fish for a lunch stop at one of the roadside parks ahead, while enjoying views of Lake Michigan.

Another roadside attraction in the area is the Garlyn Zoo, located about 6 miles east of Naubinway. The zoo is home to a lot of rescue animals native to North America, along with exotic animals from around the world. The friendly atmosphere created by the owners contributes to the overall enjoyment of the visit, as they allow guests to get up close with the animals. The woodsy setting of the animal habitats blends in well with the Upper Peninsula environment. It's a nice way, and totally unexpected for this part of the country, to spend an afternoon.

Don't worry if your visit to the zoo runs late and you don't have a place to stay. The Hog Island Point State Forest primitive Campground is just a mile away on US 2. This is another rustic campground, with vault toilets and potable water. It also has a beach area where you can rinse off the day's road grit.

A couple miles east of the town of Epoufette, be sure to allow time for a stop at the Cut River State Roadside Park. At least pause a few moments to enjoy the view from the bridge over the river. On one side of the bridge you can see where the Cut River empties into Lake Michigan, while the other side offers open views down into the deep gorge the river has cut into the limestone bluffs. I'm sure if you stop to enjoy the view you will also choose to hike the long stairway that leads down to the river. You can then follow a trail along the river bank to the mouth of the river and shore of Lake Michigan. It's a nice hike, and you can hike the opposite river bank trail on your return to the bridge. On the slow steep climb back up the stairs, you will have plenty of time to admire the steel structure of the bridge. Construction of the bridge was delayed in 1941 to divert steel for the war effort.

Alright, you've been seeing advertisements for them along the ride all across the Upper Peninsula, so if you haven't yet tried a pasty, or even if you have been munching on them for the past few days, be sure to stop and feast on one from Letho's Famous Pasties. It's just a small unimpressive-looking roadside structure, located about 6 miles west of St. Ignace, but their homemade version of the tasty treat is as good as any I've had. The original owners, who operated the store since its beginning in 1947, have recently sold the business, however the new owners say they have no intentions of changing any of the process.

A pasty is described as a pot pie without the pot. It is made by placing uncooked filling, typically of meat and vegetable, on a flat pastry, then folding the pastry around the filling and baking. I heard the long history of the food staple from a local, about how the miners in Cornwall, England used to pack the pasties with them down into the mines, and then heat them in the scoop of a shovel over a candle.

The people of the Upper Peninsula take their pasties seriously. So whenever you stop for one of the treats, be sure to ask the maker about the ingredients and their own special recipe for making them.

While riding the final stretch of US 2 on the approach to St. Ignace, I caught a nice tailwind coming off the lake. With sand dunes on both sides of the highway and the waves of Lake Michigan lapping up on the beach, I was once again reminded of cycling along the west coast.

There is a nice roadside park, located across from the National Forest Information Center, with an unobstructed view of both the Straits of Mackinac and the Mackinac Bridge. Perched high on a bluff overlooking the lake, the park provides a great photo op.

As the third oldest continuously inhabited settlement in the United States, St. Ignace has a wealth of historic sites and museums. These sites tell an interesting story that began some fifty thousand years ago, when the original natives summered in the area, to being the seat of authority of New France, then as a possession by the British following the Seven Year War, and finally to became a territory of the United States as a result of the American Revolutionary War. To collect information about the area attractions, visit the St. Ignace Visitor Bureau, located at 6 Spring Street Suite 100, 906-643-6950.

Continue riding along US 2, past numerous motels and over the I-75 entrance to the bridge, until you reach the Mackinaw Island Information and Ferry Ticket office. It is housed in a small building that is modeled after a lighthouse. You can stop at the office to inquire about where you want to go from here. You basically have two options for crossing the Straits of Mackinac, and neither option involves riding your bicycle because bicycles are not allowed on the bridge. Bummer!

Option one: take a ferry to Mackinac Island, then another ferry to Mackinaw City. Note: see the following section for an optional visit to Mackinac Island.

Option two: Shuttle across the Mackinac Bridge via the Mackinac Bridge Authority.

If you choose option one, follow the directions at the ticket office to reach the dock for your selected ferry. You should also pickup a chunk of Murdick's Fudge for the trip, located across from the dock. I recommend the dark chocolate.

For option two, backtrack on US 2 for less than a mile, crossing over the I-75 automobile entrance to the bridge, and turn left on Boulevard Drive. Follow this road for .6 mile, then turn left on Densmore Avenue to ride another .1 mile to reach a parking area for the state police. You then cross the parking area to reach the pedestrian bridge over I-75 to the Mackinac Bridge Authority building. You will have to carry your bike up/down three flights of stairs. This is where the shuttle across the bridge begins. Cost of the shuttle is $5.00 per bicycle. If you have additional questions about the shuttle, the bridge authority can be reached at 906-643-7600.

Before crossing the bridge, at the left turn onto Densmore Avenue, you can continue straight to visit Bridge View Park, where videos and displays tell the interesting story about the construction of the bridge and the challenges posed by the Straits of Mackinac. The park also offers a great view of this, the 12th longest suspension bridge in the world, at 3.64 miles long.

View of the Mackinac Bridge from Bridge View Park, the 12th longest suspension bridge in the world. Impressive!

Camping

Milakokia Lake SF CG	*Michihistrigan CG & Cabins	Black River SF CG
Milakokia Lake Rd	W17838 US 2	Black River Rd
Gould City, MI	Gould City, MI	Naubinway, MI
906-293-5131	906-477-6983	906-477-6048
		(3 miles Black River Rd)

*Hog Island Point SF CG
US 2
Naubinway, MI
906-635-5281
(7 miles east Naubinway)

*Lake Michigan Rec CG
3701 US 2
Moran, MI
906-292-5549
(5 miles East Brevort)

Lakeshore Park CG
W1234 Pte. LaVarbe Rd
St. Ignace, MI
906-643-9522
(1 mile off US 2)

Lodging

*Dreamland Motel
1520 W US 2
Gulliver, MI
906-283-3122

*Scheall's Motel
W19210 US 2
Gould City, MI
906-477-6462

*Laidlaws Ctry Corner Motel
W16495 US 2
Gould City, MI
906-477-8092

*Hog Island Ctry Cottages
W8294
Naubinway, MI
906-477-9995

*Bay View Inn
W5961 US 2
Epoufette, MI
906-292-0061

*Brevort Motel
W4385 US 2
Brevort, MI
906-292-5488

*Thunderbird Inn
10 S State St
St. Ignace, MI
906-643-8900

*Aurora Borealis Inn
635 US 2
St. Ignace, MI
906-643-7488

*Voyager Inn
W750 US 2
St. Ignace, MI
906-643-1530

Bike Shops

N/A

Gulliver to St. Ignace (72 miles)

Miles N/S	Directions	Dist	R	Service	Miles S/N
0	L at SS on US 2	9.6	3	LQ	72.0
10	S on US 2	5.6	3	CLQR	62.4
15	*Gould City				56.8
15	S on US 2	15.4	3	CLQR	56.8
31	*Naubinway			GLQR	41.4
31	S on US 2	9.2	3	CGLQR	41.4
40	*Hog Island				32.2
40	S on US 2	5.7	3	CL	32.2
46	*Epoufette Bay			CGLQR	26.5
46	S on US 2	5.7	3	C	26.5
51	*Brevort)			CLQR	20.8
51	S on US 2	15.4	3	CLR	20.8
67	S on US 2	5.4		CLR	5.4
72	*St Ignace			CLQR	0

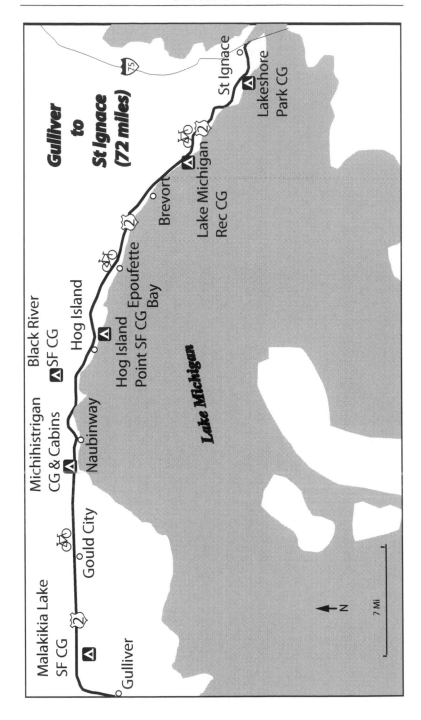

Gulliver
to
St Ignace
(72 miles)

St Ignace

Lakeshore
Park CG

Brevort

Lake Michigan
Rec CG

Epoufette
Bay

Black River
SF CG

Hog Island

Hog Island
Point SF CG

Michihistrigan
CG & Cabins

Naubinway

Lake Michigan

Malakikia Lake
SF CG

Gould City

Gulliver

N

7 Mi

98

Lake Michigan Trail
OPTIONAL TOUR

Mackinac City to Mackinac city (8 miles)

When you buy your ferry ticket in St Ignace, go ahead and buy a round trip ticket, even though you will not be returning to St Ignace. You can buy a one way to the island then another one way from the island to Mackinaw City, but it cost a little more. So buy a round trip for you and your bike, and then you can use the other half of that round trip ticket when you leave the island to continue on to Mackinaw City. The tickets are color coded, so someone may approach you to say you are in the wrong line, but just tell them you meant to be in that line. They will be good with this. At the time of this printing the price for a round trip ticket was $25 per person and $9 per bike/trailer. A tandem bike requires two tickets.

The ferry ride from St Ignace to Mackinac Island is a little over 15 minutes, and about the same time from Mackinac Island to Mackinaw City.

If you visit in February you won't be dependent on a ferry to reach the island. You can use the "ice bridge", which is available once the lake has frozen over. It's about a 3 mile ride and the "ice bridge" route is bordered by Christmas trees lining the designated route. If you do make the trip to the island in the winter months you will experience what locals refer to as the "Hidden Season".

As the ferry approaches the island the Grand Hotel really stands out among the other structures. It is enormous.

The ferry will drop you off on Main Street, right in the heart of the shops, gift stores, restaurants, and hotels. While you're there, you might want to stop off at the Mackinac Island Tourism Bureau, located at 7274 Main Street, to pick up maps and other information to help you plan your visit.

When first planning for the trip, like everyone else, I had heard about there being no automobiles on the island, but until I actually arrived on there I didn't know what it would be like to not be sharing the road with cars.

Initially I was reminded of being in a downtown area where selected streets have been blocked off for pedestrian or bicycle use only. So this was not a totally unfamiliar environment. Then, I began walking around the downtown district of Mackinac Island, along with all the other people, and at times I was able to ride my bike among the crowds of people. But then, when I left the busy downtown district behind the crowds begin to thin out, and then all I saw were people on bicycles. And this was on a state highway not a bike path. Now that was something I haven't experienced.

It takes a while to adjust to not having motorized vehicles around. For the longest time I kept watching for cars at intersections and glancing over my shoulder before making a left turn. But gradually it begins to sink in that bicycles rule in this world. Hands down, bikes beat walking, and even horse drawn carriages, as the best way to see the island.

The island gives visitors an opportunity to see what it would be like to tour a Victorian town of the 19th century era. However, the buildings and homes in this area are not typical of the average small American communities in the country at that time.

In the post-Civil War industrial age, Mackinac Island became a favorite vacation destination for visitors from Detroit, Chicago, and other nearby industrial cities. To accommodate these guests both boat and railroad companies constructed fine hotels, restaurants, and souvenir shops.

The cottages located high on the bluffs were built by wealthy Midwestern industrialists who wanted to spend more time on the island during their summer visits. So this wasn't your average small town village of that period.

With the growing demand for more development by businesses and residents, luckily 80% of the island was owned by the government so there weren't a lot of areas available for them to build on. So, from the beginning development was limited. And in the early 1870s, when congress was concerned about the ongoing disappearance of America's finest national treasures, with the laws they passed to preserve our national parks and other government lands, Mackinac Island fell under the umbrella of other government lands, so this too contributed to its preservation.

Since that time there have been other measures passed pertaining to the island that helped preservation even further, such as requiring that all private development in the park, and that by leaseholders, maintain the original distinctive Victorian architecture.

In 1898, when the new-fangled "horseless carriage" began to arrive on the scene and frightened the horses of carriage tours operator, the Mackinac Island Village Council banned automobiles from its streets. So this too helped preserve that slower tempo present at the turn of the century that visitors continue to experience to this day.

So when you are dodging all the horse poop on the streets, don't bad mouth the horses. Instead thank them for the large role they played in making the island completely bike friendly.

If you are hungry when you arrive on the island there will be plenty of opportunities on Main Street to find whatever food tickles you taste buds. Once you have had you fill to eat, you'll probably be more than ready to leave the congestion of Main Street behind. Automobiles or not, it gets pretty congested on the island in the summer months.

So pick up a chunk of fudge and begin riding out in either direction on Main Street to begin circumventing the island. I mentioned fudge because locals call tourists "fudgies" because a fudge shop is pretty much a mandatory stop for visitors. So I'm a "fudgie." I've been called worse, and besides it's good fudge and it makes for a nice snack on the ride.

The ride around the island along Lake Shore Drive is a little over 8 miles long. It follows the shoreline offering some fantastic views across the waters of Lake Huron. It also passes several interesting limestone formations from when the glaciers passed through the area some 11,000 years ago.

One of these formations that you will want to stop at is Arch Rock. If you are riding around the island on Lake Shore Drive counter clockwise, about a mile out of town you can see the arch on the bluff at the left side of the highway. If you would like a closer look, you can turn left on Rifle Range Road to hike up to the arch.

There is no way you can to rush your ride around the island, even if you wanted to. Although it is only a little over eight miles in distance, sharing the highway with a lot of other sightseeing cyclists is going to slow you down, a lot. So just take it easy and enjoy the views.

It wasn't until I was out of downtown area that it really began to sink in that there were no automobiles. Riding on a wide open highway without cars was an experience that I was not accustomed to. But, it's something that I could get used to very easily.

After circling the perimeter of the island there are many other sites to visit within the interior of the island. I do have a couple recommendations listed below of places to visit. However, with the information you collected from the tourist bureau you might prefer selecting your own sites. Either way, I hope you check out more of the island.

The Grand Hotel is pretty much a must see. You had a sample of its grandeur from the view from the ferry on the way in, now it's time to get up close and personal with it. There is nothing like it that I have seen.

Fort Mackinac is another attraction where you might want to spend some time. The fort served as a sentinel over the Straits of Mackinac for 115 years. In its fully restored original condition, with the marching soldiers, cannon blasts, and other routine activities of military life of that era, history comes to life for visitors.

Mackinac Island will tempt you to spend more time there than you had originally planned, if doing nothing more than just meandering among this well-preserved historic sanctuary for cyclists. When you are ready to leave, head back to the ferry for a short shuttle back to the mainland, in Mackinaw City.

Camping

N/A

Lodging

Grand Hotel
286 Grand Ave
Mackinac Island, MI
800-33GRAND

*Cawthorne's Village Inn
1384 Grand Ave
Mackinac Island, MI
906-847-3542

*Harbor View Inn
6860 Main St
Mackinac Island, MI
906-847-0101

*Main Steet Inn & Suites
7408 Main St
Mackinac Island, MI
906-847-6530

*Bicycle Street Inn & Suites
7416 Main St
Mackinac Island, MI
906-847-8005

*Lake View Hotel
7452 Main St
Mackinac Island, MI
906-847-3384

Lodging continued

Pontiac Lodge	Cloghaun B&B	Lilac House B&B
1376 Hoban St	7504 Market St	7337 Market St
Mackinac Island, MI	Mackinac Island, MI	Mackinac Island, MI
906-847-3364	906-847-3885	906-847-3708

Bike Shops

*Mackinac Wheels	*Mackinnac Bike Barn	*Ryba's Bicycle Rental
6929 Main St	7422 Main St	7463 Main St
Mackinac Island, MI	Mackinac Island, MI	Mackinac Island, MI
906-847-8022	906-847-8026	906-847-3208

Bicycles are the preferred mode of transportation on Mackinac Island.

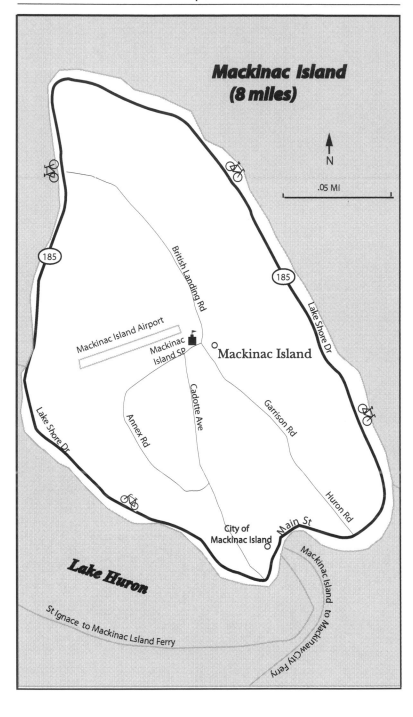

Lake Michigan Trail
SECTION 14

Mackinaw City to Bay Shore (59 miles)

If you choose the shuttle from St Ignace, you will be dropped off at a Shell station, just after crossing the bridge. Then follow the directions in the Mileage Log to merge with the other route within half-a-mile.

For those cyclists who are riding the LMT counterclockwise, there is a call box located across Interstate 75 from the Shell station, at the Audie's Restaurant. Using this phone you can call the Mackinac Bridge Authority and they will drive over to shuttle you across the bridge to St Ignace. To reach the call box, at the intersection of Central Avenue and Nicolet Avenue, just ride north a couple blocks on Nicolet Avenue.

Those arriving via boat from Mackinac Island, the ferry will dock at Huron Avenue at the end of Central Avenue. The LMT then heads up Central Avenue. This road is the main tourist strip. As you cycle along the avenue you will have plenty of options for eating and shopping, or just walking around and stretching your legs.

Several of the lodging facilities listed in the guidebook are located on Huron Avenue. If one of these is your destination, to reach them, turn right on Huron Avenue and ride about half-a-mile to find your home for the night. The Baymont Inn & Suites is located immediately across from the turn onto the bike path, so that is another convenient option.

There are a lot of interesting attractions in Mackinaw City. There is the Colonial Michilimackac, a reconstructed 1715 French village, and Fort Michilimackac, an 18th-century French fort and trading post. Then Historic Mill Creek, a rebuilt 1700s dam and sawmill, and The Old Mackinac Point Lighthouse, a restored 1800s lighthouse and watch keeper's lodgings. The city has done a great job to help recreate the atmosphere of the interesting history of the area.

If you do decide to spend some time in the area, you can pick up more information at the Mackinaw Area Tourist Bureau, located at 10800 US 23.

Regardless of which option you chose to cross the straits, the two routes merge at the intersection of Central and Nicolet Avenues. The entrance to the bike path is one block south of this intersection. Once cruising along the separated bike path you quickly leave the busy activities of Mackinaw City behind.

There is a convenience store located at the turn onto Cecil Bay Road. You can also continue straight another 4 miles to reach the Wilderness State Park Campground. The park has 26 miles of beach along the Lake Michigan shoreline, camping, rustic cabins, and a bunkhouse.

The LMT through here routes cyclists through good old Michigan backcountry and along sandy beaches. It also passes a few wetland areas, a good environment for watching for wildlife. I saw a turkey while riding through here.

The community of Cross Village was named after a large cross planted by Father Marquette in approximately 1675. There is a replica of the cross in a grassy meadow overlooking Lake Michigan.

The lodging and restaurant listed for Cross Village is at the Legs Inn. There is a historic marker telling the interesting story behind this unique structure that makes it well worth a visit.

Immediately after leaving the village, the LMT routes cyclists through a section known as The Tunnel of the Trees. For the next several miles hardwoods and evergreens crowd the edge of the pavement, truly creating a tunnel for you to cycle through. I thoroughly understand why this stretch of road has been ranked among the most scenic in the state of Michigan.

Have I overused the phrase, "this is a great ride?" Once you've ridden it you will agree that you can't overuse the phrase when describing numerous sections of the LMT.

The restaurant I indicate in the Mileage Logs in Good Hart is a small deli/general store, with an emphasis on small. But I did enjoy a bowl of fresh homemade soup of the day here.

There is also an interesting log cabin located next to the deli that houses Primitive Images. This is an antique shop that also houses a tea room, and during the tourist season they have a trailer outside serving delicious crepes. The 1840 hewn log cabin was moved down from Quebec. The nice ladies running the shop have some interesting stories to tell about the cabin and the unique furnishings they have on display. I know you won't be shopping for furniture while bicycling through here, but it is an interesting stop.

Be sure to watch for the turn onto Lower Shore Drive. State Highway 119 continues straight and it is an easy turn to miss.

Harbor Springs lays claim to having the deepest natural harbor in all the Great Lakes. The quaint town retains a lot of the distinctive architecture from the 1800s, during the peak of their fishing and lumber era. It also has Yummies Ice Cream & Yogurt, located at 220 E. Main Street, very appropriately named.

You can exit town with a left on Main St (State Highway 119) to ride 1.9 miles to the trailhead of the Little Traverse Wheelway (LTW), but the LMT follows a more scenic route recommended by area cyclists, to join the LTW later. You also pass a nice lake shore park on this route that is a good place to stop for a break.

Shortly after the LMT joins the LTW, as it parallels State Highway 119, it passes the entrance to Petrosky State Park. Following this, the LTW veers away from the busy highway so cyclists can leisurely meander along the lakeshore.

As the LTW emerges onto Lake Street it passes under an arch sign stating, "No Teaming or Driving". This dates all the way back to the 1800s when the bikeway was first built, when people were prohibited from riding horses or driving horse-drawn carriages on the trail. It's amazing that this trail predates the railroad. Petrosky was truly ahead of its time.

You can find more about the history of the trail by visiting the Little Traverse History Museum, located at 100 Depot Street. You can also learn about the Ernest Hemingway connection with Michigan at the museum. Hemingway has always been one of my favorite authors, but I wasn't aware of his connection with Michigan.

After a short ride on Lake Street the LMT routes you back on a separated bike path. Magnus Park is also located at this turn. This is the city-owned public campground that offers camping on the banks of Lake Michigan. A perfect setup for bicycle tourists.

I have a feeling there were several bicyclists on the Smithsonian Institute committee that rated Petrosky as one of the top 20 small towns in the United States.

The LTW is great at routing cyclists away from the congestion and traffic along US 31, however, if you are in need of supplies, food, or lodging, you can turn left at the Hampton Road crossing for a good selection.

107

The Old Mackinac Point Lighthouse and lightkeepers dewelling. Began operation in 1892. The light was visible to ships sixteen miles away.

Camping

Mill Creek CG
9730 US 23
Mackinaw City, MI
231-436-5584

Wilderness SP CG & Cabins
903 Wilderness Park Dr
Carp Lake, MI
231-436-5381

Petrosky KOA
1800 N US 31
Petrosky, MI
231-347-0005

*Petrosky SP
2475 M-119 Hwy
Petrosky, MI
231-347-2311

*Magnus Park CG
901 W Lake St
Petrosky, MI
231-347-1027

Lodging

Super 8 Bridgeview
601 N Huron Ave
Mackinaw City, MI
231-436-5252

Lighthouse View Motel
699 N Huron Ave
Mackinaw City, MI
231-436-5304

Riveria Motel
520 N Huron Ave
Mackinaw City, MI
231-436-5577

American Boutique Inn
517 N Huron Ave
Mackinaw City, MI
231-436-5543

*Baymont Inn & Suites
109 S Nicolet St
Mackinaw City, MI
800-337-0550

*Legs Inn & Cottages
6425 N Lake Shore Dr
Cross Village, MI
231-526-2281

*Birchwood Inn
7291 S Lake Shore Dr
Harbor Springs, MI
563-357-5467

Coach House Inn
1011 N US 31
Petrosky, MI
231-347-8281

Terrace Inn
1549 Glendale
Petrosky, MI
800-530-9898

Bike Shops

Touring Gear
108 Third St
Harbor Springs, MI
231-526-7152

High Gear Sport
1171 N US 31
Petrosky, MI
231-347-6118

North Country Cycle Sports
410 Howard St
Petrosky, MI
231-487-1999

Latitude 45 Petrosky
476 W. Micthell
Petrosky, MI
231-348-5242

Mackinaw City to Bay Shore (59 miles)

Miles N/S	Directions	Dist	R	Service	Miles S/N
	Route for those who took the ferry				59
0	S on Central Ave	0.3	4		59
0	L at SL on Nicolet St		3		59
	Route for those who were shuttled				59
0	L out of Shell Station on Jamet St	0.1	2	Q	59
0	L at SS on Louvigny St	0.1	2		59
0	L at SS n Central Ave	0.1	3		59
0	R at SL on Nicolet St, where option 1 and 2 merge	0.1	3	G	59
0	R on unamed bike path	1.2	P		59
2	R at SS on Trails End Rd	1.3	2		57
3	S at SS on Headlands Rd/Wilderness Park Dr	3.5	2		56
6	L on Cecil Bay Rd	3.6	2	Q	53
10	R at SS on Gill Rd	3.1	3		49
13	R on Lakeview Rd	2.8	3		46
16	L on Lake Shore Dr	6.3	3		43
22	*Cross Village			LQR	37
22	S on Lake Shore Dr/SH 119	7.6	2		37
30	*Good Hart			R	29
30	S on Lake Shore Dr/SH 119	5.6	2		29
35	R on Lower Shore Dr	3.5	2		24
39	R at SS on Lakshore Dr/SH 119/Lake St	3.2	3	LR	20
42	*Harbor Springs	0.1		GLQR	17
42	R on State St	0.7	3		17
43	L at SS on Bay St	0.5	3		16
43	R at SS on Zoll St then L on Beach Rd	1.1	3		16
45	R at SS on Pennsylvania Ave	0.3	3		15
45	L at SS on Beach Rd	2.5	3		14
47	R on Little Traverse Wheelway (LTW)	5.2	P	C	12
52	*Petoskey			CGLQR	7
52	R on Lake St	0.2	2		7
53	R on LTW	6.4	P	CQ	6
59	*Bay Shore			Q	

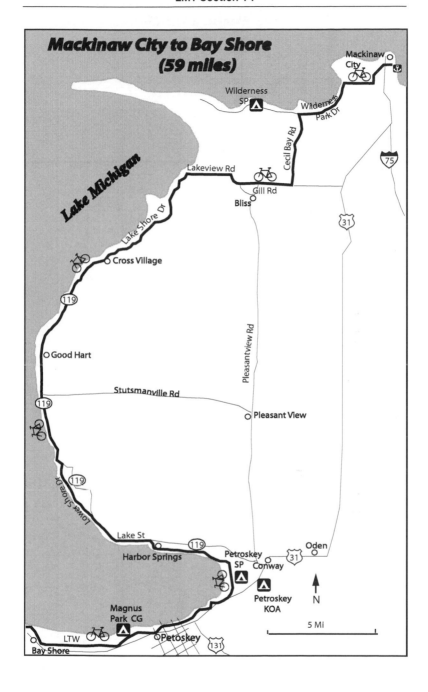

Mackinaw City to Bay Shore
(59 miles)

111

Lake Michigan Trail
SECTION 15

Bay Shore to Elk Rapids (50 miles)

The LTW leads you into the first few miles of this section. Then it follows a few back roads to reach the town of Charlevoix. Just after crossing the bridge over Round Lake, you have the opportunity for a side trip that I highly recommend. It is only about half-a-mile off the LMT so you might as well go for it.

Turn right on Park Avenue and ride the triangle of streets (Park Avenue, West Clinton Street, and Grant Street) that circle the world renowned "mushroom houses". Earl Young began creating the structures within this block in 1918. Often referred to in print as hobbitland, elf spaces, and gnome homes, the houses have a whimsical fairy tale appearance.

Like Andrew Lloyd Wright, Young believed that houses should blend in organically with their surroundings. Young employed liberal amounts of stone in the structures, some being very large stones, and used curved cedar shake for the roofs. At times the roofs come so close to touching the ground that the windows have to be cut through the roofs. Young once said that he liked to build the roof first, then shove the house under it.

I hope I've teased your imagination enough to make the short ride to check out these unique houses. Interesting attractions like this are a bonus on a tour.

As you ride through Charlevoix on Bridge Street, you pass the visitor information. You might want to stop here first to pickup more about the history of the mushroom house to better appreciate your tour. You can also visit the American Man Cave store on Bridge Street. I had to stop just to see if my man cave was properly furnished.

After leaving Charlevoix the LMT routes cyclists back into the scenic countryside, with rolling hills and farm houses. Then you tour the shores of Torch Lake. The name was derived from the Native American practice of lighting torches at night on the lake to harvest fish with spears and nets.

Most of the homes through this area appear to be vacation homes. I like it when the residents post names for their houses, it gives them instant character. It seems like it would be more practical to build seasonal homes on lakes like Torch Lake than Lake Michigan to avoid the storms.

I saw a healthy red fox cross the highway as I was riding through this area.

After leaving Kewadin, be sure to continue across US 31 on Williams Road before making the left turn on Bayshore Drive. It would be easy to assume the directions meant to turn on US 31.

With US 31 running in the same direction as the roads the LMT follows through this area, what traffic there is, the drivers shouldn't be in a hurry. If they were they would be on the more wide open US 31.

The later stretch of this section routes you through a number of large healthy fruit orchards. Keep your eyes out for roadside produce stands so you can pick up fresh food for road snacks.

The Mileage Log for this section extends a few miles south of Elk Rapids, even though I list the town as the end of the section. Sometimes the cities just don't fall where you need them for the maps.

BTW, Elk Rapids was named after a set of Elk horns that were found in the Mguzee Rapids. It was previously named Stevens. I wonder how Stevens felt about this?

Camping Section 15

Fishermans Island SP
16480 Bells Bay RD
Charlevoix, MI
231-547-6641

Barnes Park CG
12298 Barnes Park Rd
Eastport, MI
231-599-2712

Honcho Rest CG
8988 Cairn Hwy
Elk Rapids, MI
231-264-8548

Lodging Section 15

*Edgewater Inn
100 Michigan Ave
Charlevoix, MI
231-547-6044

*The Lodge Motel
120 Michigan Ave
Charlevoix, MI
231-547-6565

Maple Leaf Motel
1414 Bridge St
Charlevoix, MI
231-547-0057

Lodging Section 15 (continued)

*Torch Bay Inn
4871 US 31
Eastport, MI
231-599-2412

*Cairn House B&B
8160 Cairn Hwy
Elk Rapids, MI
231-264-8994

Camelot Inn
10962 US 31
Williamsburg, MI
231-264-8473
(just south Elk Rapids)

Bike Shops Section 15

Revolution Bike & Board
102 Mason St
Charlevoix, MI
231-237-0900

Earl Young's famous "Half House" in Charlevoix. One of the series of series of mushroom homes he built.

Bay Shore to Elk Rapids (50 miles)

Miles N/S	Directions	Dist	R	Service	Miles S/N
0	*Bay Shore			Q	50
0	S on LTW	5.5	P		50
6	R on Waller Rd	1.1	2		44
7	L at SS on McSauba Rd	0.6	3		43
7	R at SS on Division St/Michigan Ave	0.4	3		43
8	VR at SS on Petroskey Ave/Michigan Ave/Bridge St/US 31	0.6	3		42
8	*Charlevoix			GLQR	42
8	R on Antrim St	0.1	3	G	42
8	L on State St	0.7	3		42
9	R at SS on Bridge St/ US 31	1.0	4	R	41
10	L on Barnard Rd	6.7	3		40
17	S at SS on Norwood Rd/4th St	2.1	3		33
19	*Norwood				31
19	L on Gennett Rd	0.2	3		31
19	R on Dixie Hwy	6.5	3		31
26	L at SS on Zore Rd/Old Dixie Hwy	0.3	3		24
26	*Eastport			Q	24
26	R at SS on US 31	6.1	3	CQR	24
32	L on Barnes Rd	0.9	3		18
33	VR on Torch Lake Dr	7.5	3		17
40	R on Indian Rd	2.2	3		10
43	L at SS on Cairn Hwy	0.1	3		7
43	*Kewadin			GL	7
43	R at SS on Cairn Hwy	0.4	3		7
43	R on Williams Rd	1.0	3		7
44	L at SS on Bayshore Dr (after crossing US 31)	2.4	2		6
46	R at SS on Dexter	0.3	2		4
47	*Elk Rapids			CGQR	3
47	L at SS on River St then R on Bridge St	0.6	3		3
47	L at SS on 4th St then after crossing US 31 R on Green St	0.2	3		3
48	BL at SS on Elk Lake Rd	1.9	3		2
49	R on Townline Rd/ CR 605	0.5	2		1
50	R on Townline Rd/ CR 605		2		

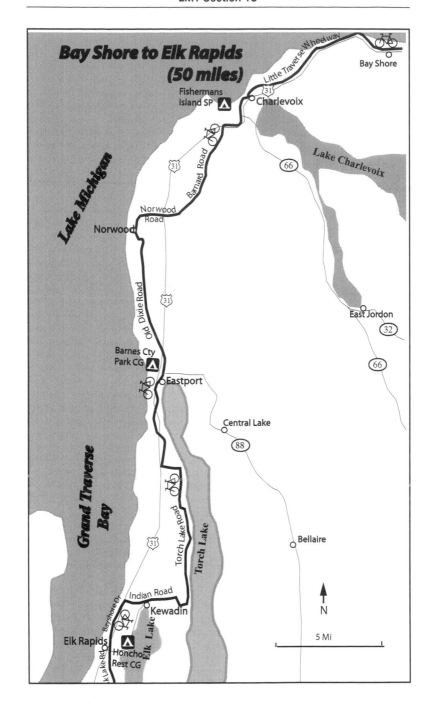

Bay Shore to Elk Rapids
(50 miles)

Lake Michigan Trail
SECTION 16

Elk Rapids to Glen Arbor (58 miles)

When you're riding along Angell and Bates Roads watch for the fields of sunflowers. Others have told me they are really great, but I guess they haven't been in bloom when I've been through here.

There is a short stretch of the Traverse Area Recreation Trail (TART) at the beginning that is separated from the rest of the trail. I was visiting with a local cyclist during a break on the trail and he told me there is a section of abandoned railroad that will eventually link this isolated section with the rest of the trail, but there are a lot of politics involved that is holding it up.

I'm not going to say anything bad about Michigan politics. From what I've seen, they could be used as a model for other states to follow on the subject of creating a more bicycle friendly environment.

As you are riding the roads connecting the two sections of TART, on Bunker Hill Road make sure you don't follow the bicycle sign for Vasa Trail. That is a mountain bike trail. Just continue on Bunker a little further. The entrance to TART is just before you reach US 31.

Immediately after beginning this section of the TART, the path will take you directly behind the Crestwood Motel. There is a social trail leading from the bike path to the motel, making it very convenient to stop here. Ride a little further and you'll find another social trail leading to the Bay View Inn, which is a restaurant that serves up a plate of tasty fresh fish caught daily in Traverse Bay.

A lot of businesses have realized what an opportunity it is to have the TART running near their business, because you will also pass social trails leading to a general store, ice cream shop, and the Traverse City State Park. What a great setup this area is for cyclists.

When the TART comes to a T-intersection at Woodmere Avenue, you cross the highway then turn right. You can also follow signs at this intersection to reach the library.

Just after you've made the right turn, you pass an old railroad station that has been converted into a brewery & pizza place. I know, you're asking yourself, "Can it get any better than this?"

Continuing along the path, the TART ducks under a bridge under US 31, and then circles around to take you over this same bridge. Just after this the bike path enters Clinch Park. This is a nice park, with restrooms, picnic tables, a marina, and 1500 feet of sandy beaches.

There is also a must see statue known as "Time to Let Go", by artist Verna Bartnick. The art work depicts an adult pushing a small child on a bicycle. The adult is running behind and he can just barely touch the bicycle seat. It's obvious the child is ready to try to ride on their own, but the parent doesn't want to let go.

As I sat sipping on my water bottle, reflecting on this inspiring work of art, I realized this is true of life in general. Sometimes you just have to let go and work your way through whatever follows. Kind of like when the day you began your ride around Lake Michigan. You made sure your bicycle was in good condition, you found some place to stash your gear on the bike, you bought this guidebook (thank you), and then finally one day you decided whatever else you needed you would either pick up on the tour or do without it.

This stretch of the TART is directly across from downtown Traverse City. Anywhere along here you can cross US 31 to find a place to eat or tour around the historic district. The Traverse City Tourism Center is in this downtown area at 101 West Grandview Parkway. So gather information on this interesting city and spend some time here.

Keep an eye out for when the TART crosses over to the other side of the highway. It would be easy to miss because there is another paved path that continues straight on the bayside of the highway. Match the distance for the turn in the Mileage Log and watch for when US 31 turns away from the bay. This is your crossing.

After crossing the four lane highway, which becomes State Highway 72 after the intersection, the TART continues to parallel State Highway 72 a short distance, now on the east side, before veering off to the left. Just before the TART leaves, there is a large grocery store located conveniently alongside the trail, so you can pick up any needed supplies before heading off into the country.

And when I say off into the country I mean it. Almost immediately you are riding past farms, wetlands, orchards, nature preserves, and rural countryside. It's a relaxing atmosphere for cycling, but use caution at the highway crossings.

By the way, after leaving Traverse City the bike trail you are riding is actually the Leelanau Trail. With the goal of creating a stronger force for recreation and alternative transportation, the trail groups in the Traverse City area united to form TART Trails, Inc., a 501(c)3 nonprofit and list all the trails under the TART name. Like I mentioned earlier, Michigan could be a model for other states to follow.

You can turn left off the TART at the Bingham Road crossing and ride about a tenth of a mile to take a break and check out the old 1877 Bingham Schoolhouse. Not much to see but it is a convenient place to get off the bike for a while.

As you are approaching Sutton Bay, at the 4th Street crossing, you can turn right to ride about a block to reach a grocery store and deli.

The LMT takes you right through downtown Sutton Bay on Joseph Street. There are a variety of places to eat through here, such as the Village Inn, the oldest tavern in the county, established in 1865. The Guest House B&B is also conveniently located on Joseph Street, if you are ready to stop for the night. And then there is my favorite stop, the Ice Cream Factory.

On State Highway 204, about 3 miles out of Sutton Bay, you pass a right turn to a veterans memorial park. The park is only about a tenth of a mile off the LMT. It is a nice setting to pause a moment to pay your respects to those who paid the ultimate price to protect our freedom.

The LMT routes you through some really healthy looking grape vineyards. Among these rows of vines you pass a turn for Blustone Winery. It is only about half a mile back to their tasting room, which is located in the middle of their vineyard with a view across the fields of grape vines. A little further along your ride you pass the Good Harbor Winery. With the tasting room right along the roadside it is very convenient to stop for a taste, and possibly select a bottle for your evening camp.

You might also want to pick up a pastry to go along with your wine at the Covered Wagon Market & Bakery, located at 8996 East Duck Lake Road. Sweets and wine, I don't know. Maybe get some cheese and crackers instead.

The restaurant I have flagged on Manitou Trail is Market 22. This combination deli, liquor outlet, pizzeria, and market is operated by the Kokowicz, father and son partnership. This is the kind of local business that is run by nice people, that I really like to support.

On your approach to Glen Arbor the LMT passes the entrance

to the Port Oneida Rural Historical District. If you ever wanted to know what it would be like to be bicycle around in a turn of the century Midwest farming community, this is about the best opportunity you're going to find. With 121 buildings, 20 structures, and 18 farmsteads covering over 3,400 acres of farming area, preserved as it was in the late 19th century, it makes for a really enjoyable bike tour.

If you are planning to camp at the end of the section, the DH Day campground is located just south of Glen Arbor.

Bronze sculpture "Time to Let Go", by Verna Bartnick, located in Traverse Citysw.

Camping

*Traverse City SP	Wlld Cherry Resort CG	*DH Day CG
1132 US 31	8563 E Horn Rd	8000 Harbor Hwy
Traverse City, MI	Lake Leelanau, MI	Glen Arbor, MI
231-922-5270	231-271-5550	231-33404634

Lodging

*Crestwood Motel	Sleep Inn & Suites	Borders Inn & Suites
5200 US 31	5520 US 31	1870 US 31
Acmew, MI	Acme, MI	Traverse City, MI
231-938-2670	231-938-7000	866-599-6674
Holiday Inn	*Guest House B&B	*Jolli Lodge
615 E Front St	504 Joseph St	29 N Manitou Tr
Traverse City, MI	Sutton Bay, MI	Lake Leelanau, MI
800-315-2621	231-271-3776	888-256-9291

Bike Shops

Einstein Cycles
1990 N US 31
Traverse City, MI
231-421-8148

Brick Wheels
736 E 8th St
Traverse City, MI
213-947-4274

McLain Cycle
750 N 8th St
Traverse City, MI
213-941-7161

One of a Kind Cycle
630 Cottageview Dr
Traverse City, MI
866-734-6990

Elk Rapids to Glen Arbor (58 miles)

Miles N/S	Directions	Dist	R	Service	Miles S/N
	R on Townline Rd/ CR 605				58
0	L on Munroe Rd	2.0	3		58
2	R at SS on Angell Rd	0.9	3		56
3	L on Bates Rd	3.1	3		55
6	R at SS on Hawley Rd/Bates Rd	0.5	3		52
7	L at SS on Bates Rd	1.0	3		51
8	S at SS to cross SH 72 to begin Traverse Area Rec Tr (TART)	1.7	P		50
9	L on Lautner Rd	0.4	3		49
10	R on Bunker Hill Rd	1.7	3		48
11	*Acme			CGLQR	47
11	L on TART/Leelanau Tr	5.8	P		47
17	S at SS to cross Woodmere Ave then R on TART	1.9	P	R	41
19	*Traverse City				39
19	L at SL to cross US 31 then R on TART	15.6	P	G	39
35	*Sutton Bay			GLQR	23
35	S on Cedar St/St Joseph St	0.5	3	R	23
35	L on Race St/SH 204/Duck Lake Rd	3.9	3		23
39	*Lake Leelanau			GQR	19
39	S on Phillip St/Duck Lake Rd	3.2	3		19
42	L at SS on Manitou Tr/SH 22	6.4	3	LR	16
49	S on Harbor Hwy/River Rd/SH 22	9.2	3		9
58	*Glen Arbor			CGLQR	

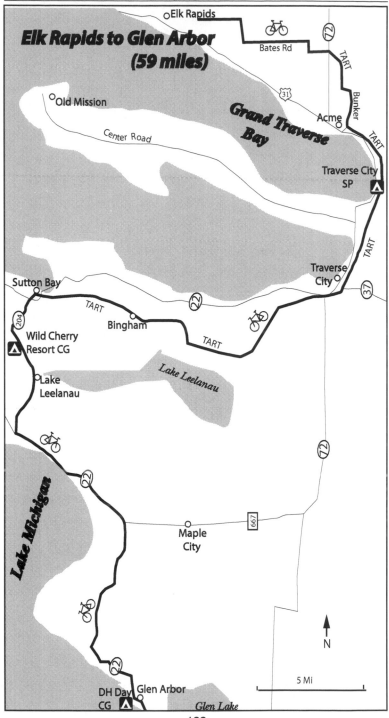

Elk Rapids to Glen Arbor
(59 miles)

Grand Traverse Bay

Elk Rapids

Bates Rd

72

TART

US 31

Bunker

Acme

TART

Old Mission

Center Road

Traverse City SP

TART

Traverse City

Sutton Bay

TART

Bingham

TART

22

37

204

Wild Cherry Resort CG

Lake Leelanau

Lake Leelanau

72

Lake Michigan

22

Maple City

667

22

N

5 Mi

22

DH Day CG

Glen Arbor

Glen Lake

Lake Michigan Trail
SECTION 17

Glen Arbor to Onekama (57 miles)

In Glen Arbor, State Highway 22 turns left and the LMT continues straight on State Highway 109, but for just a short distance. You get to leave the busy highways behind you for a little while as you take advantage of the newest completed segment of the Sleeping Bear Heritage Trail (SBHT).

The last time I came through here the SBHT ran from Glen Arbor to Empire, about 10 miles. However, at that time they already had plans for a new section to extend the bike path north of Glen Arbor, with it eventually stretching all the way to the northern boundary of National Lakeshore. When finished, the SBHT will total 27 miles of hard-surface multi-use trail.

Currently the completed section of SBHT conveniently routes cyclists pass the DH Day Campground, through Historic Glen Haven, and then to the Dune Climb. Glen Haven is a restored logging village situated within the Sleeping Bear Dunes National Lakeshore.

There are several impressively preserved buildings in the village for you to stroll around and checkout. There is the DH Day general store (now serving as a ranger station), the Glen Haven Canning Co building (currently housing the Cannery Boathouse Museum), and the Sleeping Bear Inn. No, unfortunately the Inn is no longer in operation, however, they say if you close your eyes and shutdown all your senses but your sense of smell, you can still inhale a faint aromatic whiff of the butter and syrup laden pancakes they were so famous for.

When you have finished your sightseeing in Historic Glen Haven, before heading back on the SBHT, continue through the village another half-a-mile to visit the Sleeping Bear Point Coast Guard Station Maritime Museum. This is the original U.S. Life-Saving Station that was moved here when the dunes were beginning to bury it in sand at its previous location. You'll hear a lot more about how active the sand dunes are during your visit at Sleeping Bear.

At the museum you learn about the important role the U.S. Life-Saving Service played in the history of shipping on the great lakes. Following the winter of 1870-71, when 214 people lost their lives in shipwrecks on the Great Lakes, Congress appropriated the money to develop professionally trained rescue crews. These crews were then strategically stationed along the shores of the lakes to assist in recuses of vessels in distress.

During the summer months there are daily re-enactments at the museum of procedures the crews used to rescue shipwreck survivors. It's nice that we have these exhibits around to preserve our heritage and bring it to life for visitors to experience.

On the second floor of the museum there is also a reconstructed Steamer Wheelhouse that offers a panoramic view of the Manitou Passage.

The SBHT next routes you past the Dune Climb. This is a 260 foot sand dune that the Park encourages people to hike up. This may not sound that tall but the tallest sand dune on the Atlantic Coast is only 100 feet. So park your bike to show off your level of fitness and knock out the Dune Climb.

There are restrooms and a gift store located at the base of the dune.

Once you exit the Dune Climb parking lot you are back on the SBHT for a fun ride over some nice rolling hills all the way to downtown Empire. Sweet!

Along this section of the SBHT you pass the Stocking Pierce Scenic Drive. This is a beautiful 7.4 mile loop that takes you through dense forest, sand dunes, and grand views across Lake Michigan. At the information exhibits along the loop you also learn the noble tale of how Pierce Stocking built this road to share the beauty of the area with others. What a nice guy.

It's a very scenic loop and all, but for those who are touring on a bike, just passing through the area, I just can't recommend taking it. A lot of the loop is over rolling hills, and with a fully loaded bike, it isn't much fun. Now if you are staying in the area for a few days and have your bike with you, sure, by all means ride the loop. I mean, this scenic tour is the type of attraction that you lug your bike on a vacation for.

Empire promotes itself as "The Most Beautiful Place in the World". Quite a claim to fame, but I'll let you decide. Maybe if you stop at the Grocer's Daughter Chocolate store it might sway your opinion. There is also a museum and visitor center in town.

After leaving Empire you have an enjoyable ride ahead over a smooth surfaced tree lined road, with a nice 3-foot shoulder. Not bad at all. You are riding along the shoreline of lakes other than Lake Michigan. I know Minnesota is known for having a lot of lakes, but based on the number of lakes the LMT routes you pass, Michigan has to be a close second.

It is only a half-mile ride off the LMT to reach the Platte River Campground.

As you enter Frankfort, continue straight at the flashing street light onto 7th Street. At the stop sign for Main Street, the LMT crosses to enter the library parking lot, and then turns left to begin the Betsie Valley Trailway. This paved bike path runs along the banks of Betsie Lake, another beautiful lake. The library is convenient if you want to check your email.

I can remember when you rode miles out of your way to find a library to check your email. Now all you need is cell coverage. I'm not sure if this accessibility is a good thing?

While still in Frankfort, after about 1.5 miles, the Betsie Valley Trailway crosses Lake Street to parallel River Road. The LMT turns right at this crossing, off the bike path, to follow Lake Street. If you are ready to camp, you can continue on the bike path another mile to reach the Betsie River Campground listed in the guidebook. But, once again, the LMT leaves the bike path and turns right.

About 8 miles out of Frankfort the LMT passes a roadside park that offers a great view of the shoreline of Lake Michigan. There are stairs that will take you higher for an even better view. There are restrooms here also.

As you leave Arcadia you get to ride the first of the notorious Three Sisters Climbs. They aren't as steep coming from the north, but it's still a noteworthy ascent for the LMT, and the descents are an adventure all their own with a fully loaded bike.

You know the fruit they sell at the roadside produce stands is fresh through here because the orchards are all around the stand.

As you approach Onekama, it's kind of a tradition to turn right on Portage Point Rd and ride about half-a-mile to drink some of the refreshing waters of the artesian well at Little Eden Christian Retreat. I'm a sucker for traditions like this, but it's your call if you want to drink untreated water.

The "Dune Climb". A 260' sand dune located in Sleeping Bear, located in Sleeping Bear Dunes National Lakeshore.

Camping

*US Platte River CG
5685 Lake Michigan Rd
Honor, MI
877-444-6777

Betsie River CG
1923 River Rd
Frankfort, MI
231-352-9535

Arcadia Marina CG
17220 First St
Arcadiaw, MI
231-794-1854

Lodging

Lakeshore Inn
5793 S Ray St
Glen Arbor, MI
231-334-3773

*Duneswood Cottages
7194 Hwy 109
Empire, MI
231-688-6789

Lakeshore Inn
11730 S Lacore Rd
Empire, MI
231-326-5145

*R&R Motel
541 Lake St
Frankfort, MI
231-352-9238

*Wayfarer Lodgings
1912 S Scenic Hwy 22
Frankfort, MI
800-735-8564

*Sunset Valley Motel
18726 Burnham Dr
Arcadia, MI
231-889-5987

Lodging (continued)

*Pleasant Valley Motel
17229 6th St
Arcadia, MI
231-889-4194

*Portage Lake Motel
4714 Main St
Onekama, MI
231-889-4921

*Travelers Motel
5606 8 Mile Rd
Onekama, MI
231-889-7076

Bike Shops

N/A

Glen Arbor to Onekama (57 miles)

Miles N/S	Directions	Dist	R	Service	Miles S/N
	*Glen Arbor			GLQR	
0	S on Western Ave/SH 109	0.1	3		57
0	L on S Forest Haven Dr	0.3	2		57
0	R on Sleeping Bear Heritage Trail (SBHT)	1.3	P		56
2	S to cross SH 109 resume (SBHT)	0.8	P	C	55
3	*Glen Haven	0.0			54
3	S on (SBHT)	2.3	P		54
5	VL to cross Dune Climb parking lot	0.2	P		52
5	R to cont on SHBT	5.5	P		52
11	*Empire			QR	46
11	S on SH 22	21.5	3	CQ	46
32	*Frankfort			GLQR	25
32	S at SL on 7th St	0.1	3		25
32	L on Betsie Valley Trailway	1.5	P		25
34	R on Lake St the L on Frankfort Ave/SH 22/Scenic Hwy	12.1	3	R	23
46	*Arcadia			CGLQR	11
46	S on SH 22	10.9	3		11
57	*Onekama			GLQR	

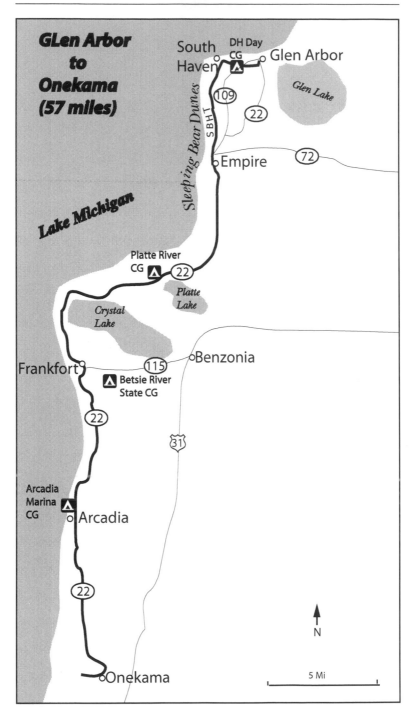

GLen Arbor to Onekama (57 miles)

South Haven

DH Day CG

Glen Arbor

Glen Lake

109

22

Sleeping Bear Dunes

S B H T

Empire

72

Lake Michigan

Platte River CG

22

Platte Lake

Crystal Lake

Benzonia

Frankfort

115

Betsie River State CG

31

22

Arcadia Marina CG

Arcadia

22

N

5 Mi

Onekama

Lake Michigan Trail
SECTION 18

Onekama to Hart (64 miles)

You have a lot of camping opportunities in this section to select from. Many of the ones listed in the guidebook border the LMT. Orchard Beach State Park is one of them, offering a convenient welcome setting for cyclists to pitch their tent. Located on a bluff overlooking Lake Michigan you have a great vantage point for watching the evening sun as it sinks on the horizon into the lake's boundless waters.

After leaving Onekama the LMT routes you through several lake resort areas. There are stretches on some roads where lakeshores border both shoulders of the highway. I can't explain why, but for no particular reason it just felt like a bike friendly area.

The town of Manistee has a very impressive historic district. The city has taken several of the well preserved older buildings and turned them into museums.

One reason there are so many striking older buildings in the town is that at the time the city suffered a devastating fire in 1871, the area was profiting from a major lumber boom. As the result of this prosperity, in the 1880s Manistee had the largest number of millionaires per capita than anywhere else in the Unites States. So, they had plenty of money to rebuild.

An interesting side note about the Manistee fire is that it was one of five major fires in the Midwest that occurred on the date of October 8, 1871. In addition to this one, there was the Great Chicago Fire, the Great Peshtigo Fire, the Holland Fire, and the Port Huron Fire. Although the Chicago Fire was the most famous, the Peshtigo Inferno, with between 1,200 and 2,500 associated deaths, was far more lethal. This was the most deadly fire in Unites States history.

There is not a lot of traffic after leaving Manistee, but without a shoulder I still rate it a 3. You are back out in the country again, with large plowed fields, farm houses, truly away from the cities. I hope you have a tailwind when riding through here because you are really exposed at times, what with the open plowed fields.

The Lake Michigan Recreation Campground is about 8 miles off the LMT. That's a long way to ride out of the way, but this is located on the shores of the lake and really gets you back in the

woods. I wouldn't normally include a campground this far from
the LMT in the guidebook, but I thought everyone would see the
signs for the campground and I want my readers to know how far
it is off the route.

As you enter the town of Lundington, the right turn in the
Mileage Log onto Stearns Drive takes you through Stearns Park.
The park has restrooms and picnic tables, and it's right on a public
beach, so it makes for a good place to stop for a break. If you would
rather bypass the park, you can choose to remain on Lakeshore
Drive to reach the next turn listed in the guidebook.

Be sure to stop for a meal, or at least desert, at the House of
Flavors, located at 402 West Ludington Avenue. The restaurant is
a 50's-style diner, which is pretty cool in itself, but the main reason
for stopping is the ice cream. It is prepared at the House of Flavors
plant, which is located directly behind the restaurant. With all the
mementos dating back to 1948 when they began as a dairy, it's a fun
place to visit and the food is tasty, too.

As you are riding along Dowland Street, you can make a left
turn on Maritime Drive to reach the SS Badger Ferry. As I said
earlier, when we were on the opposite bank of Lake Michigan, if
you don't have the time to ride the entire LMT the ferry is a great
way to split it up into two separate loop tours. Hop on the ferry to
make the 60-mile cruise across the lake, and four hours later you
are back at the vehicle you left on the other side at the start of the
ride.

I liked using the ferries on the MRT to create loop tours.
Ferries are a lot of fun and it is a unique mode of travel.

There wasn't a street sign for the Pere Marquette Highway
turn when I last came through here. After the turn you will see
signs calling it PM Hwy. The traffic is pretty busy on this road but
there is a shoulder.

At the left turn off Iris Road onto Lakeshore Drive, if you turn
right and ride a mile you reach the Butterville Campground listed
in the guidebook. The park is located on a bluff overlooking Lake
Michigan.

You ride past the Historic White Pine Village on your way to
the campground. This is a village with over thirty museum buildings
and sites preserving Mason County's past. It captures the authentic
small town atmosphere of Michigan life in the 1800s.

Rolling along atop the bluffs on Lakeshore Drive you pass some
very nice views across Lake Michigan. There is one view that was so
impressive that it was worth the highway department building a
pedestrian crosswalk over the highway to reach it.

You pass a B&B along this stretch, but it stands for Beef & Bees. Funny!

You also pass Bortell Fisheries. This is a sixth-generation business that serves freshly caught fish. They prepare it both fried and smoked, and give you a choice of coleslaw and fries, or both. They even have picnic tables outside where you can eat. This is a must stop for a bicycle tourist. I recommend the smoked salmon. Bortell is located right on the LMT.

This is a relaxing ride along Lakeshore Drive, with winding roads bordered by pine forests. There isn't much traffic, but keep an eye out for what vehicles there are.

Pentwater has a reputation for being a beacon for artists from all over the Midwest. It does seem to have a creative free spirited atmosphere about it. I passed a couple roller-blading down the main street, and I mean right in the middle of the road, and motorists didn't seem to mind. Check out the gingerbread-decoration on many of the quaint shops.

The LMT routes cyclists around the shores of Pentwater Lake past nice cottages bordering the lakeshore.

When you reach Hart, if you continue on Main Street a few more blocks past the LMT turn onto Water Street, and you reach State Street you will find a good selection of eating places, grocery stores, and the Hart Motel listed in the guidebook.

I have to say something about the Hart Motel. First, it is a very clean well maintained older motel, and second, it is truly a unique place to stay. The rooms have kind of a mountain lodge décor to them. There are fire rings on the grass lawns in front of the rooms, with stacks of firewood provided to encourage guests to gather in the evening. It is definitely an interesting place to stay. Tell Bret you read about the motel in my guidebook and maybe he will upgrade you to a room with a hot tub.

To make this even more perfecte, there is an IGA grocery store right across the street in front of the motel and the Hart-Montague Trail runs right behind it.

Camping

*Orchard Beach SP
2064 Lakeshore RD (Hwy 22)
Manistee, MI
231-723-7422

Lake Michigan Rec CG
Forest Trail 5629
Manistee, MI
231-723-0141
(8 miles off LMT)

*Cartier Park CG
1254 N Lakshore Dr
Ludington, MI
231-845-1522

Buttersville CG
991 S Lakeshore Dr
Ludington, MI
231-843-2114

*Whispering Surf CG
7070 S Lakeshore Dr
Pentwater, MI
231-869-5050

*Hill & Hollow CG
8915 US 31B
Pentwater, MI
231-869-5811

Charles Mears SP
400 West Lowell St
Pentwater, MI
231-869-2051

*River Farm CG
5480 N Wayne Rd
Pentwater, MI
231-869-8127

John Gurney Park
300 N Griswold St
Hart, MI
231-873-4959

Lodging

Super 8 Motel
220 Arthur St
Manistee, MI
231-398-8888

*Little Riverside Motel
225 N US 31
Manistee, MI
231-398-3420

*Riverside Motel
520 Water St
Manistee, MI
231-723-3554

*Ventura Motel
604 W Ludington Ave
Lundington, MI
231-845-5124

*Lighthouse Motel
710 W Ludington Ave
Lunington, MI
231-843-3333

*Pines Motel
8228 US 31B
Pentwater, MI
231-869-5128

Hexagon House B&B
760 Sixth St
Pentwater, MI
231-869-4102

Hart Motel
715 S State St
Hart, MI
231-873-4000

Comfort Inn
2248 Comfort Dr
Hart, MI
231-873-3456

Bike Shops

*Trailhead Bike Shop
216 W Lunington, MI
Lunington, MI
231-845-0545

Onekama to Hart (64 miles)

Miles N/S	Directions	Dist	R	Service	Miles S/N
	*Onekama			GLQR	64
0	S on SH 22	2.7		QR	64
3	R on Cresvent Beach Rd	1.8	3		61
5	VL on Lakeshore Rd/SH 110	7.3	3	C	59
12	*Manistee			GLQR	52
12	R on Veterans Oak Grove Dr	0.5	3	LR	52
12	L at SS on Washington St/Maple St	0.8	3		51
13	R on Water St	0.6	2		51
14	R at SS on 1st St	0.2	3		50
14	L on Cherry Rd	1.7	3	R	50
16	R at SS on Red Apple Rd	3.7	3		48
19	L at SS on County Line Rd	1.6	3		44
21	R on Quarterline Rd	6.5	3	C	43
27	R At SS on Townline Rd	0.5	3		36
28	VL on Stiles Rd	2.1	3		36
30	R at SS on Fountain Rd	2.2	3		34
32	VL on Angling Rd	2.4	3		31
35	L at SS on Jebavy Dr	2.7	3	QR	29
37	R on Jagger Rd	2.0	3		26
39	L at SS on Lakeshore Dr/SH 116	1.7	3	C	24
41	R on Stearns Dr	0.5	3		23
42	*Ludington			CGLQR	22
42	L on Ludington Ave	0.5	3	LR	22
42	R at SL on Rath Ave	0.4	3		22
42	L on Dowland St	0.4	3	R	21
43	R at SS on Washington Ave	0.6	3		21
43	L on 6th St	1.1	3		20
45	R at SS on Pere Marquette Hwy/Marquette Dr/SH B31	1.0	4	Q	19
46	R on Iris Rd	1.5	3		18
47	L at SS on Lakeshore Dr	5.8	3	CR	17
53	R at SS US 31B/Hancock St/Monroe Rd	3.3	3	CLQR	11
56	*Pentwater			CLQR	8
56	L on 6th St/US 31B	0.7	3	L	8

57	R on Monroe Rd/US 31B	1.0	3		7
58	R on Longbridge Rd	0.4	3		6
58	L on Wayne Rd/64th St/Wayne Rd/68th Ave	3.4	2	C	5
62	L at SS on Harrison Rd	0.5	2		2
62	R at SS on 72 Ave	1.0	4		2
63	L at SS on Tyler Rd/Main St	0.5			1
64	*Hart			CGLQR	

Beautiful bluff view at reststop along Lakeshore Drive. Notice how the highway used by the LMT runs right along the bluffline.

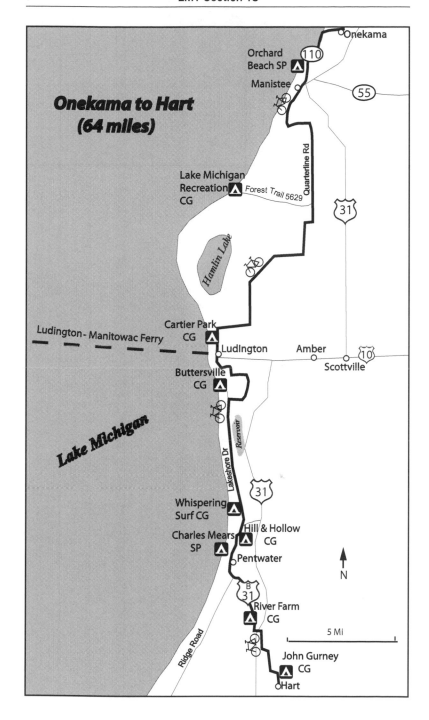

Onekama to Hart
(64 miles)

Onekama

Orchard
Beach SP
110

Manistee

55

Quarterline Rd

Lake Michigan
Recreation
CG

Forest Trail 5629

31

Hamlin Lake

Cartier Park
CG

Ludington - Manitowac Ferry

Ludington

Amber

Scottville

10

Buttersville
CG

Lake Michigan

Reservoir

Lakeshore Dr

31

Whispering
Surf CG

Charles Mears
SP

Hill & Hollow
CG

Pentwater

N

B
31

River Farm
CG

5 Mi

Ridge Road

John Gurney
CG

Hart

Lake Michigan Trail
SECTION 19

Hart to Grand Haven(63 miles)

About half-a-mile into the ride on the Hart-Montague Trail (HMT) you cross Polk Road. There is a rest area beside the trail on your left here and also Hansen Food Market. This is a nice grocery that also serves a wide selection of cooked food.

If you turn right and ride about a mile on Polk Road you reach an exit for US 31. The Comfort Inn listed in the guidebook is located here, along with an assortment of fast food eateries. However, you can also remain on the HMT and it will take you right the behind Comfort Inn.

The HMT takes you across open plowed fields, through thick forests, and past lush wetlands. This is a great environment for spotting wildlife. I remember when I was a kid, travelling with my mother in a car, and I would see long trains from the highway, crossing fields in the distance, and it looked like they were in their own peaceful world apart from the busy highways. Well, now that tranquil world is for cyclists.

About 3.5 miles into the HMT you pass the Wood Shed Bike Shop, listed in the guidebook. This is a small shop but they will be able to help with repairs and basic parts.

There is a rest area with a picnic table about 6.7 into the HMT.

It was nice to spot several black squirrels again while I was riding the HMT. I'm used to seeing grey and brown squirrels so these are more exotic for me. I love it when you are approaching them on the bike path and when they notice you coming they take off running, down the bike path the same direction you are riding. They keep running in front of you until you are just about to run over them before they realize all they have to do is step off the bike path to avoid being run over. I can see where the term squirrely behavior came from.

There is a convenience store and a restaurant as the LMT crosses State Street in Shelby. You can see them from the bike path.

As an FYI, the hardware store in Rothbury carries a few bicycle parts. I kind of get the idea that they see a few bicycles come through this area when a small hardware store carries bicycle parts.

As the HMT enters Montague you come to a fork. The HMT continues to the left, but if you remain on the paved path to the right another block you pass Twisters Ice Cream, and a grocery store. While you are enjoying your ice cream treat be sure to check out the world's largest working weather vane across the parking lot. The weather vane itself is 48 feet tall and the directional arrow is 26 feet long. Now, that's worth a taking a selfie to take send home your cycling buds.

The Trailway Campground, listed in the guidebook, is located in the middle of the fork in the bike paths. Just remember, when you have finished camping, eating ice cream, or shopping for groceries, and you are ready to resume your ride, veer left to remain on the LMT.

Shortly after leaving the fork, you cross a bridge and you reach the trailhead parking for the end of the HMT. The White River Chamber of Commerce is also located at the trailhead if you would like to pick up information about the area.

You will actually continue to follow the HMT another half-a-mile beyond the parking lot to ride through a tunnel under busy US 31. The bike path then crosses and parallels Lake Street

The LMT also passes one of my favorite stops while cycling through here, an ice cream shop. But this isn't just any ice cream. This is Pekadill's, a local tradition for over 30 years. They not only serve up 32 flavors of hand packed ice cream, they also serve a variety of unique foods. To reach Pekadill's take a left on West Sophia Street for a block and then a right on South Mears Avenue for a block and you will be there.

After returning from Pekadill's on West Sophia Street, cross Lake Street and continue on the bike path until you reach a bridge that crosses over Lake Street. The LMT veers to the right here, away from the bike path that continues straight and crosses over the bridge. Shortly after this the bike path is little more than a sidewalk before eventually you end up riding on Lake Street.

The LMT is following the shoreline of White Lake through here, for those who are keeping a tally of lakes to pass on the LMT.

At the left turn onto Scenic Drive, you can continue straight on Murray Road to ride less than a mile and a half to reach the White River Lighthouse. The lighthouse tower and keeper residence housing is now a museum that is open to the public. When you visit this castle-like structure be sure to ask the curator, Karen

McDonnell, to tell you the tale about the haunting of the former lightkeeper, William Robinson.

You might try to time your visit at the lighthouse in the late evening. The sunsets from its grounds are said to be some of the more spectacular in the world.

About 3 miles into the Scenic Drive road be sure to watch for where the road makes a right turn. It is an easy turn to miss, or I should say it was easy for me to miss this turn.

This is a great ride through here, at times you're riding right along the shoreline of Lake Michigan. A great way to top off your day would be with a stop at the Red Rooster Tavern for something to eat and drink. The tavern has been serving travelers since 1923.

The Muskegon Lakeshore Trail (MLT) makes it easy for cyclists to avoid interacting with motor vehicles while passing through Muskegon, but you might want to take a side tour to see some of the interesting sites in the downtown area. Such as the Muskegon Heritage Associate, 561 W Western Avenue, the Hackley & Hume Historic Site, 484 W Webster Ave, the Muskegon Museum of Art, 296 W Webster Ave, and the Muskegon County Visitor Center, 619 W Western Ave. You might want to start off at the visitor center to collect information about these sites.

There are some stretches of wooden boardwalks on the MLT, so use caution, because these can become slippery when wet.

The MLT routes cyclists past the shoreline, industrial areas, marinas, and it also conveniently passes Fisherman's Landing & Campground, listed in the guidebook.

Upon reaching McCracken Street and leaving the LMT, you can turn left on Lakeshore Drive to visit a hot dog stand and various art venues. You could also turn right on Lakeshore Drive to ride 3 miles to visit the Great Lakes Naval Memorial & Museum.

A half mile into McCracken Street, at the Sherman Boulevard intersection, if you are in the mood for some really great comfort food at a fair price, you can turn left to visit the Cherokee Restaurant. You can see it from the intersection. Or you can continue a little further on Sherman for your choice of fast food.

A block before exiting McCracken Street on Seminole Road, you can turn left on Norton Avenue and ride another mile and a half to reach the Seaway Motel, listed in the guidebook. This is on an exit for US 31, and there are also other motels to choose from in this area.

After leaving Muskegon, keep an eye out for the various

stretches of separated bike trail and painted bike lanes. I encourage cyclists to utilize these whenever possible because motorists get upset sometimes when you ride on the highway when there are bike paths available.

When you reach the end of 3rd Street, cross Pine Street and then turn right to enter Ferry Park. The bike path passes through the park then veers right to travel under State Highway 104. It then parallels US 31 on a bridge with a protected separated bike lane. This will take you over Grand River. Once across the bridge, turn left to follow the sign to Harbor Island. Almost immediately, the bike path ends and you turn left on Island Harbor Drive to ride back under US 31 once again. There is no street sign here.

Once you pass under the highway the LMT routes you through a recreation area, and pass some porta-potties for a quick pit stop. Watch for the rough railroad crossing on Coho Drive.

You are now in Grand Haven.

Camping

Lucky Lake CG
3977 W Wilke Rd
Montague, MI
231-893-9608
(about 2 miles off HMT)

*Trailway CG
4540 Dowling St
Montague, MI
231-894-4903

*Muskegon State Park
3560 Memorial Dr
Muskegon, MI
231-744-3480

*Fisherman's Landing & CG
538 E Western Ave
Muskegon, MI
231-726-6100

PJ Hoffmaster SP CG
6585 Lake Harbor Rd
North Shores, MI
231-798-3711

Lodging

*Weathercane Inn
4527 Dowling St
Montague, MI
231-893-8931

*Michillinda Lodge
5207 Scenic Dr
Whitehall, MI
231-893-1895

White Lake Motel
305 E Colby St
Whitrehall, MI
231-894-4526

*Sunset Beach Cottages
1403 Scenic Dr
North Muskegon, MI
231-744-5333

Causeway Motel
440 Whitehall Rd
Muskegon, MI
231-744-1612

Seaway Motel
631 W Norton Ave
Muskegon, MI
231-733-1220

Washington St Inn B&B
608 Washington St
Grand Haven, MI
616-842-1075

Rodeway Inn
1010 @ Beacon Rd
Grand Haven, MI
616-846-1800

Harbor House Inn
114 S Harbor Dr
Grand Haven, MI
616-846-0110

Bike Shops

*Wood Shed Bike Shop
1669 N 56th Ave
Mears, MI
231-873-4338

The Bicycle Rack
1790 Roberts St
Muskegon, MI
231-773-6411

Breakway Bicycle
4741 Harvey St.
Muskegon, MI
231-799-0008

Breakway Bicycle
215 N Ferry St
Grand Haven, MI
616-844-1199

Rock & Road Cycle
300 N 7th St
Grand Haven, MI
616-846-2800

The 1875 White River Light Station museum. Open to the public.

Hart to Grand Haven (63 miles)

Miles N/S	Directions	Dist	R	Service	Miles S/N
0	*Hart			CGLQR	63
0	R on Waters St	0.5			63
1	S at SS on Hart-Montague Trail	8.3	P		62
9	*Shelby			GQR	54
9	S on Hart-Montague Trail	4.0	P		54
13	*New Era				50
13	S on Hart-Montague Trail	3.5	P		50
16	*Rothbury	0.0		R	46
16	S on Hart-Montague Trail	6.2	P		46
23	*Montague			CGLQR	40
23	S on Hart-Montague Trail	0.5	P		40
23	*Whitehall				40
23	S on HMT	0.6	P	R	40
24	R on Lake St	1.3	3		39
25	VR on S Shore Dr	1.5	3		38
26	R on S Shore Dr	2.0	3	R	36
28	L at SS on Scenic Dr	2.2	2		34
31	R cont on Scenic Dr	7.3	3	CGL	32
38	L on Memorial Dr/Ruddiman Dr	3.4	3	R	25
41	*Muskegon				21
41	R at SS to begin Muskegon Lakeshore Trail	0.6	P	R	21
42	R to cont on Muskegon Lakeshore Trail	6.4	P	CR	21
48	L on McCracken St	1.9	3	GR	14
50	L at SS on Seminole Rd	0.3	3		12
51	R at SS on Lake Harbor Rd	3.9	3	C	12
54	VL on Pontaluna Rd	1.4	3		8
56	R on Black Lake Rd/Palm Dr	1.8	2		7
58	L on Hickory St	0.4	3		5
58	R on 180th Ave/Dogwood Dr	1.9	P		5
60	R at SS on 174th Ave/3rd St	0.7	P	G	3
61	*Ferrysburg				2
61	S to cross Pine St then R to Ferry Park then R to begin Bike Path	0.6			2
61	L on Island Harbor Dr/Grand Isle Dr	0.3	P		1
62	R on Coho Dr/3rd St	1.0			1
63	*Grand Haven				

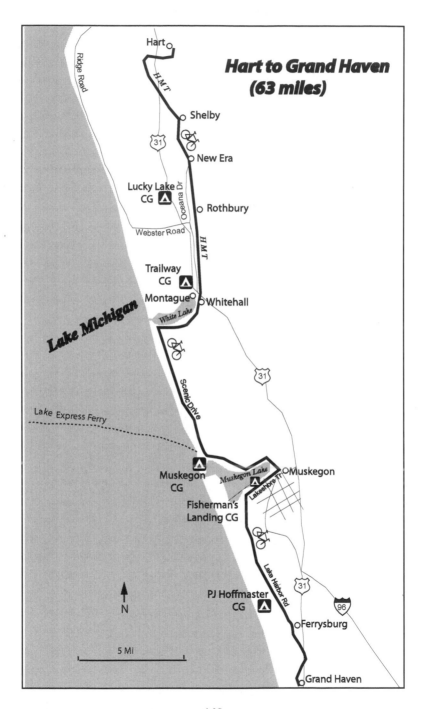

Hart to Grand Haven
(63 miles)

Lake Michigan Trail
SECTION 20

Grand Haven to South Haven (54 miles)

The Tri-Cities Historical Museum has two locations in New Haven. Both are located in the heart of the downtown district and right off the LMT. To reach them, continue straight on 3rd Street another block past the turn on Columbus Avenue, and then turn right on Washington Avenue to ride a block. The museum covers the three cities of Northwest Ottawa County: Grand Haven, Spring Lake, and Ferrysburg, so there is a lot of interesting history to learn about, both have an entrance fee that is even within my budget, free.

Since you're already on Washington Avenue, you might as well ride another 2 blocks to North Harbor Drive to see the World's Largest Musical Fountain. It is pretty impressive, with 20 minute shows nightly with accompanying synchronized water, light, and music. Having the Grand River as a backdrop really enhances the experience.

You will also want to stroll around this boardwalk area to see the big sundial, the harbor, and other points of interest.

If you spend so much time touring the area that it's late when you finish and you need to find a place to stay, not a problem. You can reach the Grand Haven State Park camping by continuing out on South Harbor Drive. In all, it is about 1.5 miles off the LMT. The park has a nice sandy beach on Lake Michigan and you can also visit the Grand Haven Lighthouse.

Grand Haven was originally a French settlement that was very big in the fur trading business. The original fur trading post was taken over by John Jacob Astor, the first millionaire of the United States. I did not know he was our country's first millionaire. You learn so much touring on a bicycle.

If you skip the side trips mentioned above but are looking for a place to eat, you can turn left off 3rd Street onto Jackson Street and ride a couple blocks where you will have a wide choice of eating establishments.

The bike path along Lakeshore Drive is the Lakeshore Connector Path (Grand Haven to Holland). It passes the Rosy Mound Natural Area. This has an interesting boardwalk across the dunes to a beach. Parts of the walk take you under a shaded canopy, a nice place to take a break and rest for a while. If you want to ride a little further before your break, about 4 miles later you pass Kirk Park, which offers a similar setting.

In the township of Port Sheldon, just after passing a large power generating plant on the lake side of the highway, Lakeshore Drive veers off to the right. The LMT continues straight on the Connector Path, to now border Butternut Drive.

There are a variety of places to eat and resupply as you ride through the town of Holland. If you are planning to camp at Drew's Country Camping, on your approach into town on Butternet Drive, turn left on Quincy Street, ride about 2.3 miles then turn left on Hallacy Drive. After half-a-mile the road will curve to become Ransom Street. You will reach the entrance to the camp after less than half-a-mile.

Riding along the Connector Path into Holland, after crossing the Macatawa River Bridge, the LMT leaves River Avenue to follow a bike path to the right paralleling Pine Avenue. If you continue a couple more blocks past the left turn onto 3rd Street, there is some interesting metal artwork displayed along the highway in front of a salvage yard. I thought it was worth riding a couple extra blocks.

In Holland you have the opportunity to visit the only authentic Dutch windmill operating in the United States. I love it when I get to visit an "only" attraction.

You can take a tour up the five stories of the windmill to see how everything operates. The mill is located in a Dutch-themed village with fields of beautiful flowers. To reach it, turn left off Central Avenue on East 8th Street and ride three blocks to turn left on Lincoln Avenue for the entrance to the village. If you would like more information about the area, you pass the Convention Center & Visitor Center on you ride to the park, at 76 East 8th Street.

Holland would be a nice place to possibly drop your panniers for a couple days to explore. The town actually does have a link to the country of Holland, as the earlier settlers were Dutch. So take the time to learn about this unique city's history.

The LMT routes cyclists through downtown Holland and past some nice older well-kept homes. After leaving Holland on 64th Street, you leave the city behind and have a nice stretch of road bordered by either a separated bike path or a wide shoulder. There are also a couple of small parks that it passes.

Saugatuck is another picturesque town that is pleasant to tour about on your bike. Douglas is also scenic, and close enough to

Saugatuck that you could visit both from one home base.

There are several establishments along the way to spend the night that are close to the LMT in Saugatuck, on and around Butler Street, but they are a little pricey. In an effort to find less expensive lodging the pair I have listed in the guidebook are just a little off the LMT. However, if you just stay on Blue Star Hwy they will be easy to find. When you are ready to rejoin the LMT just take any of the streets off Blue Star to your right and you will be back on track after a short ride.

During the stretch of the LMT outside of Douglas that follows the Blue Star Hwy, it passes the Saugatuck Brewery, if you would like to stop to sample a local brew and have something to eat.

In South Haven the LMT runs right pass the Maritime Museum, making it a convenient stop to stretch your legs.

As I mentioned, the LMT passes several lodging opportunities at the end of this section but they are pretty pricey, so I tried to list one in the guidebook that was more reasonable. But if you don't like the one I listed you will have you choice of places along the LMT in South Haven.

The only authentic Dutch windmill operating in the United States.

145

Camping

Grand Haven SP
1001 HarborAve
Grand Haven, MI
616-847-1309

Campers Paradise
800 Robbins Rd
Grand Haven, MI
616-846-1460
(.2 mile off Sheldon Rd)

Grand Haven CG
10990 US 31 N
Grand Haven, MI
616-842-9395
(2.3 miles off LMT)

Drews Country Camping
12850 Ransom St
Holland, MI
616-399-1886
(.5 mile off LMT)

Jellystone Park CG
03403 64th St
South Haven, MI
269-637-6153
(6 miles off LMT)

Lodging

*Boyden House B&B
301 South 5th St
Grand Haven, MI
616-846-3538

Best Western Beacon Inn
1525 Beacon Blvd
Grand Haven, MI
616-842-4720
(about .5 mile off LMT)

Comfort Inn
422 E 32nd St
Grand Haven, MI
616-392-1000

Best Western Plaza Hotel
3457 Blue Star Hwy
Saugatuck, MI
269-857-7178

Timberline Motel
3353 Blue Star Hwy
Saugatuck, MI
269-857-7607

The Pines Motorlodge
56 Blue Star Hwy
Douglas, MI
269-857-5211

*AmericInn Lodges & Suites
2905 Blue Star Hwy
Fennville, MI
269-857-8581

*Sand Castle Inn
203 Dyckman Ave
South Haven, MI
269-639-1110

Comfort Suites
1755 Phoenix St
South Haven, MI
269-639-2014

Bike Shops

Rock N Road Cycle
91 Douglas #180
Holland, MI
616-796-0010

Cross Country Cycle
345 Douglas
Holland, MI
616-396-7491

Velo CIty Cycle
325 S River Ave
Holland, MI
616-355-2000

West Michigan Bike & Fitness
215 Central Ave
Holland, MI
616-393-0046

Rock N Road Cycle
315 Broadway St
South Haven, MI
269-639-0003

Grand Haven to South Haven (54 miles)

Miles N/S	Directions	Dist	R	Service	Miles S/N
0	*Grand Haven				54
0	L at SS on Columbus Ave	0.1			54
0	R on 5th St	0.3		CL	54
0	VL at SS on Sheldon Rd	1.0			54
1	S at SS on Lakeshore Dr	10.3	P	C	53
12	*Port Sheldon				43
12	S on Butternut Dr	8.1	P	CGQR	43
20	S at SL on River Ave	0.6	P		34
20	VR on Bike Path to parallel Pine Ave	0.3	P		34
21	*Holland			CGLQR	34
21	L on 3rd St	0.2	3		34
21	R on Central Ave	0.9	3		33
22	R on 17th St	1.3	3		32
23	L on Shore Dr	2.4	3	R	31
26	L on 160th Ave	0.4	3		29
26	R at SS on 32nd St then L on 64th St	6.2	3		28
32	R at SL on Blue Star Hwy/CR 2	1.0	P	GQR	22
33	R on Washington Ave/Holland St	1.0	3		21
34	R on Lucy St	0.1	3		20
34	L at SL on Butler St	0.4	3		20
35	*Saugatuck				20
35	L on Culver St/Lake St	0.6	3		20
35	R at SS on Blue Star Hwy	0.3	3	L	19
36	L on Main St	0.3	3	R	19
36	*Douglas				18
36	R at SS on Center St	0.2	3	GR	18
36	L at SL on Blue Star Hwy/CR 2/68th St	3.5	3	R	18
40	R at SS on SH 89/124th Ave	0.6	3	Q	15
40	L at SS on Lakeshore Dr/70th St	0.4	3		14
41	R at SS on 123rd Ave/Lakeshore Dr/70th St	4.4	3		14
45	*Glenn			QR	9
45	VR at SS on Blue Star Hwy/CR 2	6.9	3	R	9
52	R on N Shore Dr	1.9	3	R	2
54	L at SS on Dyckman Ave	0.3	3	R	0
54	R on Williams St	0.2	3	LR	0
54	*South Haven			CGLQR	

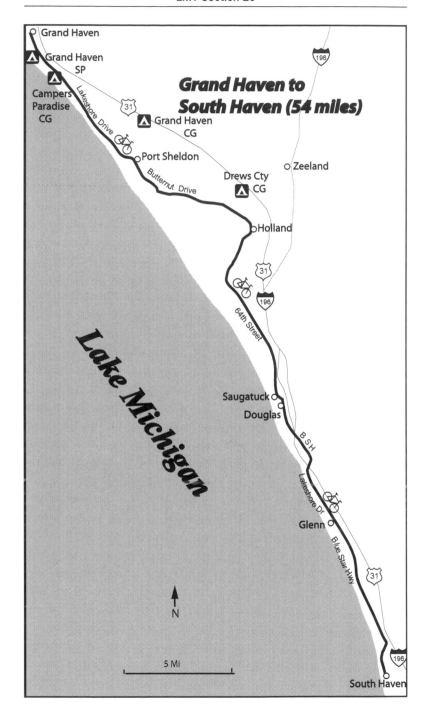

Grand Haven to South Haven (54 miles)

Grand Haven

Grand Haven SP

Campers Paradise CG

Lakeshore Drive

31

Grand Haven CG

Port Sheldon

Butternut Drive

Drews Cty CG

Zeeland

Holland

31

196

64th Street

Saugatuck

Douglas

B S H

Lakeshore Dr

Glenn

Blue Star Hwy

31

Lake Michigan

N

5 Mi

196

South Haven

196

148

Lake Michigan Trail
SECTION 21

South Haven to New Buffalo (53 miles)

If you began your tour as I did in the guidebook at New Buffalo, this is the final section of your ride. It's not a long section, so if you're not ready for your tour to be over, you'll need to make an obvious effort to slow down and stretch it out as long as possible. Stop and stroll along the sandy beaches, listen to the surf, waste some time at some tourist attraction that you wouldn't normally visit.

I have heard that when returning from a vacation, or any other extended activity, your last experience on the activity will highly influence whether the event leaves you with a fond memory or not. You could have had six enjoyable days of hanging out at the beach and on that final day it rained. That one day of rain will affect your feelings about the entire trip and you will feel that you didn't enjoy it. So keep this in mind on your last day of the tour and have some fun, because I don't want anyone to have a bad memory of the LMT.

After leaving South Haven and you are on the Blue Star Highway once again, ride for about 2.5 miles and you pass a turn for Ruggles Road on your right. If you turn here and ride another 1.6 miles you reach Van Buren State Park, listed in the guidebook for camping. Ruggles Road is not a through road, so keep in mind that you will have to backtrack to resume your LMT adventure after spending the night there.

On various stretches on the Blue Star Highway in this section, it routes you along the lakeshore past beaches with public access points. Any of these would be a good place for you to spend some time like I was talking about. Park the bike and just sit on a sandy beach for a while or take a short walk and drag your toes behind you in the soft fine granules of sand. Soak it all in, this is your last day before you have to head back to the so-called real world.

You still have an opportunity for a wine tour also, or that would be one more tour for some of us, before the end of the LMT. There are several wineries in this area but they are a few miles off the LMT. But that just means you will get to pick your own route to create your own wine tour. Or you can just stop in St Joseph to sample some area wines at the White Pine Winery Tasting room, which is only three blocks off the LMT, located at 317 State Street.

As you are approaching the St Joseph River Bridge, be sure to veer right to utilize the bike lane across the bridge into St Joseph. Once across the bridge and riding on Port Street, just after crossing the intersection with State Street (turn left for wine tasting), watch for the separated bike path on the right, paralleling Lake Boulevard. The bike path doesn't run the length of Lake Boulevard but it is nice while it last.

As you cross Broad Street be sure make a detour to your right. There are several areas of interest in this three block stretch of road that you should see.

First item of interest is the Silver Beach Carousel. This is an old fashion musical carousel similar to the one that operated on the beach here back in 1910. The carousel band organ is one of the organs that was used at the original carousel. Visit this beautiful carousel and read about the work and commitment the community has put in to bring a carousel back to their beach.

After visiting the carousel continue on to romp and play at St Joseph's Silver Beach. It is a fine wide beach and plenty of water frontages for you to play in the surf. Discover why Delta Airlines named it one of the top ten "Best Beaches in the World".

Following your fun in the sun, on your ride back to the LMT stop at the large impressive whirlpool compass fountain and play in the jets of water with the rest of the kids, also to rinse the sand off your body before climbing back on the bike.

If you are ready to eat after your water activities, you'll have plenty of opportunities to stop for something at one of the outdoor dining venues along Lake Boulevard. The area has a pleasant park like atmosphere and is a nice area to stop for a while.

If you are not up for a full meal, at the turn onto Lakeshore Drive you can stop for ice cream at the Dairy Korner. As you can tell by now, I like my ice cream while cycling. I picked it up from my bike touring bud, Bob Cable. Ice cream is a great way to replenish the large number of calories you burn while touring. Plus it taste good.

Lakeshore Drive offers more beautiful bluff views over Lake Michigan. This is a great stretch to cruise along on as you approach to the end you LMT Adventure. I paused at one of the bluff parks through here to reflect back over my ride. I also took a few more pictures here in hopes that one of them might do the view justice.

After exiting busy Lakeshore Drive, the LMT routes you along several neighborhood streets with a 25 mile speed limit, justifying the rating of a 2. Even when the rating is bumped up to a 3, it is a low end 3 and it is still a nice ride. The stretch passes several more public beach accesses for still another opportunity to bid farewell to the great lake before finishing your adventure.

The LMT passes the Grand Mere State Park along this section, however regretfully there is no camping allowed.

There is a good size produce stand along Red Arrow Highway after passing Warren Dunes State Park, plus some Mom & Pop eating places. Seeing these older businesses you are reminded that this area has been catering to visitors for a long time. Luisa's Café is a good example, serving hungry travelers since 1932. It also has an adjoining Swedish Bakery that serves up some tasty pastries. There is an outdoor dining area here, too.

When you leave Red Arrow Highway for a final time, the first sign calls the road Lake Shore Road, two words, however later the signs call it Lakeshore Road. I mention this to let you know that the names are interchangeable at this time. I don't want someone stressing out worrying if they are on the correct road when they see the name change.

Also, at the stop sign about a mile later, be sure you turn right to continue following Lakeshore Road and not left on Lakeside Road. Sounds confusing but it's not.

The approach into New Buffalo is rated a 2 because the speed limits are low and the traffic isn't bad at all. Most traffic in a hurry will be using Red Arrow Highway. These roads are also signed as a bike route.

There is a mix of old and new beach homes through this area. You also pass a lot of Inns along Lakeshore Road. I tried to include some that weren't too pricey in the guidebook.

All these beach homes reminded me of a what a guy I met here told me when I first started the ride. He explained to me how the real-estate developers in this area have a long history of trying to attract investment from the Chicago population. It seems to be working because I don't think the people who live in all these beach homes are locals.

The turn onto Marquette Drive says there is no outlet, but don't let that stop you. The neighborhood put this up to discourage people in automobiles from using this road as a through road, which makes it even better for cyclists. After a short distance you come to a stop sign, for no apparent reason. Just go ahead and stop, then continue on riding past more beach areas. What a sweet finish to the LMT.

It will eventually veer left on Whitaker Street to roll over a bridge, away from the public beach, to carry you into New Buffalo, where it all began. If you did not begin your ride at New Buffalo, or else you want to do another lap around Lake Michigan, refer to the Mileage Logs at the beginning of the book for your directions.

After you finish the ride, pull your bike into Nancy's Ice Cream Shop, at 142 North Whittaker Street and order a big double scoop ice cream cone, knowing that I will be there with you in spirit enjoying my own chocolate cone, helping you celebrate your great accomplishment.

I hope you enjoyed your Lake Michigan Adventure!

Camping

*Van Buren SP
23960 Ruggles Rd
South Haven, MI
269-637-2788

Covert Park CG & Cabins
80559 32nd Ave
Covert, MI
269-764-1421
(.5 mile off Blue Star Hwy)

Dune Lake CG
80739 Cty Rd 376
Coloma, MI
269-764-8941
(.6 mile off Blue Star Hwy))

Weko Beach CG & Cabins
5239 Lake St
Bridgeman, MI
269-465-3406
(1 mile off LMT)

*Warren Dunes SP
12032 Red Arrow Hwy
Sawyer, MI
269-426-4013

Lodging

Silver Beach Hotel
100 Main St
St Joseph, MI
269-983-7341
(1 block off LMT)

*South Cliff Inn B&B
1900 Lakeshore Dr
St Joseph, MI
269-983-4881

*Bridgeman Inn
9999 Red Arrow Hwy
Bridgeman, MI
269-465-6314
(old but reasonable prices)

*Lakeside Inn
15251 Lakeshore Rd
Lakeside, MI
269-469-0600

*Gordon Beach Inn
16220 Lakeshore Rd
Union Pier, MI
269-469-0800

Garden Grove B&B
9549 Union Pieer Rd
Union Pier, MI
269-469-6346

Bike Shops

Cycle & Fitness
1507 Niles Ave
St Joseph, MI
269-983-2453

One final look before returning to the "real" world.

South Haven to New Buffalo (53 miles)

Miles N/S	Directions	Dist	R	Service	Miles S/N
0	*South Haven			CGLQR	53
0	S at SS on Kalamazoo St	1.8	2		53
2	R at SS on Blue Star Hwy	12.7	3	CGR	51
15	*Lake Michigan Beach				38
15	S on Blue Star Hwy/CR 2/SH 63	9.7	3		38
24	*St Joseph				28
24	R at SL on Port St	0.5	3		28
25	VL on Lake Blvd	0.8	3	R	28
26	R at SL on Lakeshore Dr/Red Arrow Hwy	4.1	4	R	27
30	R on Glenlord Rd	0.4	2	QR	23
30	VL on Ridge Rd	1.1	2		23
31	R at SS on Marquette Woods Rd	0.5	2		22
32	L on Notre Dame Rd/Thorton Dr	3.0	3		21
35	VR on Willow Dr	0.1	3		18
35	L on Thorton Dr	1.4	3		18
36	L ata SS on Livingston Rd	0.2	3		17
36	R at SS on Red Arrow Hwy		4	R	16
36	*Bridgeman			CGLR	16
36	S on Red Arrow Hwy/Old US 12	9.0	4	CGQR	16
45	R on Lake Shore Rd	1.2	3		7
47	VR at SS on Lakeshore Rd	3.0	2		6
50	R on Marquette Dr	2.7	2		3
52	L on Whittaker St	0.4			0
53	*New Buffalo				

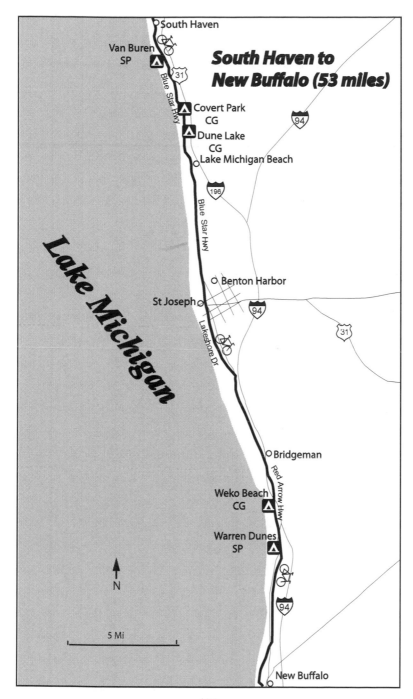

South Haven

Van Buren
SP

**South Haven to
New Buffalo (53 miles)**

Blue Star Hwy

31

94

Covert Park
CG

Dune Lake
CG

Lake Michigan Beach

196

Blue Star Hwy

Lake Michigan

Benton Harbor

St Joseph

94

31

Lakeshore Dr

Bridgeman

Red Arrow Hwy

Weko Beach
CG

Warren Dunes
SP

N

94

5 Mi

New Buffalo

Congratulations on your accomplishment!!!! Just a reminder to email me at bob@spiritscreek.com to receive your certificate of completion for bicycling the Lake Michigan Trail. As of this printing, I am very happy to announce that the governor of Michigan has also agreed to sign your certificate.

Maybe we will meet on a ride sometime to share our Lake Michigan Trail Adventures around a campfire.

Bob Robinson

INDEX

About the Author

Bob Robinson has been an avid cyclist for over 30 years. During this period he has raced both road and mountain bikes, organized races for both road and mountain bikes, built mountain bike trails, served as cycling club president, organized bicycle tours, and worked as a committee member for the National Trails Symposium. He has also ridden many extended self-supported bicycle tours. Bob knows firsthand the requirements for a safe and enjoyable cycling adventure, and designs his guidebooks to fulfill those needs.

Bob's first bicycle guidebook, Bicycling Guide to the Mississippi River Trail, has been well received by the cycling community and has sold several thousand copies in both United States, Canada, Australia, Germany, Switzerland, England, France, and other countries.

The author with the Mackinac Bridge in the background.

In research for this guidebook Bob sought input from many organizations, which he acknowledges at the front of this book, to help determine the most bike-friendly route around Lake Michigan. He looks forward to meeting cyclists, and sharing stories with them around the campfire, during his future rides on the Lake Michigan Trail, as he researches updates to the guidebook.

Made in the USA
San Bernardino, CA
31 December 2017